VISIBLE THOUGHT

This book is dedicated to David McNeill,
a true pioneer of ideas

Visible Thought

The New Psychology of Body Language

Geoffrey Beattie

Routledge
Taylor & Francis Group

LONDON AND NEW YORK

First published in 2003 by Routledge
27 Church Road, Hove, East Sussex BN3 2FA

Simultaneously published in the USA and Canada
by Routledge
29 West 35th Street, New York, NY 10001

Reprinted 2004

Routledge is part of the Taylor & Francis Group

This publication has been produced with paper manufactured to strict
environmental standards and with pulp derived from sustainable forests.

Cover design by Terry Foley, Anú Design
Typeset in Palatino by Mayhew Typesetting, Rhayader, Powys
Printed and bound in Great Britain by TJ International Ltd, Padstow, Cornwall

British Library Cataloguing in Publication Data
A catalogue record for this book is available from the British Library

Library of Congress Cataloging-in-Publication Data

Beattie, Geoffrey.
  Visible thought : the new psychology of body language / Geoffrey
Beattie.
      p. cm.
Includes bibliographical references and index.
  ISBN 0-415-30809-7 (hardcover) – ISBN 0-415-30810-0 (pbk.)
1. Body language. 2. Gesture–Psychological aspects. I. Title.
  BF637.N66B43 2003
  153.6'9–dc22
                                                                2003014530

ISBN 0-415-30809-7 (Hbk)
ISBN 0-415-30810-0 (Pbk)

Our nature consists in motion; complete rest is death.

Pascal, *Pensées* (1670)

Contents

Acknowledgements   ix

1. Introduction: *Big Brother* and other experiments   1

2. Two separate languages?   19

3. Where the action is   39

4. 'A remarkable biological miracle'   45

5. Images in the hands, images in the mind   65

6. Different vehicles of meaning   77

7. Gestures and the frustrations of everyday life   89

8. Speech is only half the story   105

9. Who or what the hands portray   119

10. A glimpse of the unguarded mind in action   141

11. Some philosophical and practical implications   175

References   196

Index   201

Acknowledgements

I would like to thank Brian Butterworth who introduced me to this area when I was a student at Cambridge and Rima Aboudan and Jane Coughlan who persevered with the work at Sheffield and Manchester. Heather Shovelton is my main collaborator in this work and she has proven herself to be an excellent researcher and collaborator and an important friend. *Big Brother* has been invaluable in generating interest in bodily communication in general and I have never failed to be impressed by the cleverness and dedication of those who work for the programme. In particular, I would like to thank Peter Bazalgette, Philip Edgar-Jones, Gigi Eligoloff, Sandra Greves, Rachel Barnes, Helen Hawken, Paul Coueslant, Walter Iuzzolino and James Christie-Miller. I would also like to thank Martin Bowley, Chief Executive of Carlton Sales, Jim Hytner, Marketing Director of ITV, Fran Cassidy, Marketing Director of Carlton Television, Tony Hopewell-Smith, Research Director of Carlton Television, and Adrian Ebery, Broadcast Research Controller of Carlton Television for their interest in the theoretical work and for urging me to see if the ideas applied to communication in the hard commercial world of advertising. David Cohen made some very useful comments on an early draft of the book. It is not usual for me to listen to such comments but his actually were spot on and I thank him for his contribution. I would also like to thank The Leverhulme Trust for their financial support.

Introduction: *Big Brother* and other experiments 1

In this book I am going to present a new theory of bodily communication, or at least of an important part of bodily communication, namely the movements of the hands and arms that people make when speaking. I will argue that such movements are not part of some system of communication completely divorced from speech, as many psychologists have assumed, rather they are intimately connected with speaking and with thinking. Indeed these movements of the hands and arms reflect our thinking, like language itself but in a completely different manner. I will argue that such behaviours provide us with a glimpse of our hidden unarticulated thoughts. Movements of the hands and arms act as a window on the human mind; they make thought visible.

This is a new theory in psychology, which owes much to the pioneering work of the American psychologist David McNeill, but as the *Big Brother* psychologist I have taken this theory and applied it to examples of behaviour from the *Big Brother* house for millions to see. Many seemed to like the basic idea and agreed that my interpretations of unarticulated thoughts were at least plausible, but what was the scientific value of this new theory? Where did the theory come from? How had it been tested? Were there other possible explanations for the unconscious movements of the hands and arms as people speak? In a television show you are not afforded opportunities to go into these kinds of issues. In this book I will outline the scientific case for this new theory and explain why movements of the hands and arms are a crucial and integral part of thinking and why careful scrutiny of these movements might reveal a great deal about the thinking of the individuals concerned and sometimes much more than they ever intended.

As the *Big Brother* psychologist my focus has been on bodily communication but now I want to argue that we may not have understood a major component of it.

It might seem odd, by the way, for a reasonably established academic to have a television programme prefixed to his occupation in this way, as in '*Big Brother* psychologist', it sounds rather like '*Blue Peter* presenter' or '*Match of the Day* pundit', but given the enormous success of *Big Brother*, that's how I am identified outside my university. *The Guardian* calls me exactly that, and sometimes I am referred to in that way inside my university as well. I sometimes find that a little strange but I am getting used to it (and no doubt one day I will simply be known as the ex-*Big Brother* psychologist, but that's a different and perhaps an even sadder story). So I now use the title, currently without the ex, perhaps a little self-consciously. *Big Brother*, after all, has been very useful in interesting the public in the micro-aspects of human behaviour, something that I have been interested in for many years, and it has provided a unique archive of material for psychologists to analyse. This archive has made a significant contribution to our thinking about language and nonverbal communication and how these two systems of communication fit together.

How has this been achieved, you might ask, when all the *Big Brother* series provide us with are highly selected individuals performing in front of the cameras? Let us not kid ourselves here. We all know how highly selected the housemates are. We have all seen the videos that they forward with their applications in their efforts to be selected for the show. The housemates are selected to achieve balance and 'interest' with one thing apparently in common – this desperate craving for fame and maybe even fortune somewhere down the line. To critics they are merely self-publicising extraverts, who know that they are continually being watched, 'acting' in front of a battery of cameras which pick up their every movement night and day. Why should such footage be of any interest to psychologists? Because, I would argue, it shows behaviour in sufficient detail in a long enough context so that we can begin to understand the individuals and to get some hint as to why they are doing what they are doing. We can then start to interpret function and motive in their communication and thereby attempt to unravel the complexity of their behaviour operating to achieve such functions in a way that no psychology experiment that I know of has ever allowed before.

Nearly all of the psychological research that has studied bodily communication in the past has been based on mere snapshots of behaviour. Small sets of individuals have been invited into a psychological laboratory, complete with one-way mirrors and hidden cameras, for short periods of time (but see the work of Albert Scheflen 1972, 1974, for a possible exception). No psychology experiment, with all of the technology necessary to record the complexity of behaviour, ever had anyone actually living in the laboratory before. But *Big Brother*, of course, did just that. The house-mates knew that they were being watched (and sometimes they acted up to the camera, pretending to freeze so that the cameramen and women might think their equipment was faulty) – but so do all participants in research in the psychological laboratory. There are strict ethical guidelines governing what participants must be told. If you are going to record behaviour with hidden cameras you should inform the participants beforehand. *Big Brother* followed these ethical guidelines.

There is another major advantage to this particular show for the psychologist in that through time in each series the audience become interested in the characters on the screen in front of them, interested in their behaviour and in their moods and their relationships, interested in what will happen to them. People are rarely interested in participants in psychological research in quite the same way. This makes the job of the psychologist that much easier. Abstract descriptions of behaviour – 'minimal eye gaze', 'high levels of self-touching in the initial period', 'open posture developing into postural echo' – became relevant to the action rather than appearing like some irrelevant academic language that misses the point of the whole thing.

Here are some examples from the third series of *Big Brother*. Kate, Spencer, Jonny, Adele, PJ, Jade, Tim, Alex, Alison, Lee, Sophie, Lyn and Sandy, their relationships and their behaviour were being discussed by the nation in the summer of 2002. One day we will probably look back and wonder why, but in that summer they gripped us. People would stop me in the street and ask, 'You're the *Big Brother* psychologist, what do you think is going on between Kate and Spencer?' I would stand there, not wishing to appear rude, rocking slightly with embarrassment, trying to say something that they had not heard before, trying to notice something for them in those layers of behaviour. I would offer up a comment and watch their reaction. 'Nah, you're wrong mate,' they would say. 'Didn't you see that look Kate gave Spencer when he chatted to Adele?' We were all psychologists now, or so it seemed.

Here were lives in miniature, for all the psychologists out there to analyse. There was meaning in the action and narratives unfolding across time to be understood and the behaviour of the characters was a clue to what was going on. It was in fact more than a clue, it was a major part of the story itself. If you missed that look, that gesture or that shrug, you didn't get it at all. Every week I travelled down to Bromley-by-Bow and later to the Elstree studios in Borehamwood to sit in front of the 'quad split', with four streams of image coming at me simultaneously in a room laden with props for the various challenges. The pressure was on for me to make my observations. The fact that the monitors were all quite small made this sometimes a difficult and painstaking task. 'Have you found anything yet?' the producer would ask. 'No pressure really, but the cameraman is set up and ready.'

The first observation I report here is about Kate, popular from the start and, in fact, the eventual winner of *Big Brother 3*, but at one point her position in the house looked decidedly shaky. This was my discussion of why that might be the case. I have prefaced each extract with the short title used in the programme itself. These were dreamt up by the producers and usually made me smile.

Kiss me Kate

From the start Kate has been a very popular housemate. She has many of the physical attributes that might suggest that she would be a big hit in the *Big Brother* house. Kate has formed very close ties with Spencer. Indeed some of the most apparently intimate moments so far in the *Big Brother* house have been between Spencer and Kate. But what is perhaps most revealing isn't what is present but what is absent. These absences might suggest that this relationship is less about love and emotion and more about protection and power. Notice how she touches his knee, they intertwine their legs and she flirtatiously touches her lips. But also notice what is missing here: although they look in the direction of the other there is actually no eye contact. Eye gaze is used here to monitor the response of the other person rather than to display real affection or any emotion towards the other person. When people are being naturally intimate they often synchronize the timing of small movements, and this is done at a very unconscious level, this is called interactional synchrony. But there is none of this interactional synchrony here.

Kate also displays very similar intimacy behaviours towards Alison. The very close interpersonal distance, sitting on her knee, the arm around her. These are exactly the same kinds of behaviours she displays towards Spencer. This again suggests that Kate might be displaying these intimacy behaviours as a strategic or political tool to build alliances within the house with powerful allies. Or people that she thinks will be powerful allies.

But Kate's got a problem. She might have chosen these allies wrongly. Alison's nomination suggests that she might not be quite as popular as Kate thought. Spencer doesn't seem to be responding to Kate's advances. What's more he refuses to be the protector that Kate wants. Not only is Kate not getting what she needs from her chosen mates, these relationships have been alienating the other housemates. Kate is now realising that her position in the house is not as secure as she'd hoped.

Here we can focus on eye gaze and interactional synchrony, or rather the absence of interactional synchrony, but these are no longer dry academic descriptions of small aspects of behaviour but an essential part of the story itself, significant clues as to what is going on in the action. The public were interested in this relationship on the screen and now they were focusing on these micro-behaviours that might hold the key to how it might develop. These micro-behaviours were slowed down and paused and isolated for them to see some of the essential elements of human social interaction. It seemed to me sometimes that we were now educating a society of people watchers.

Big Brother, of course, has a number of essential components. One is the nomination process, where each housemate nominates two other housemates for eviction and gives the reasons for their nomination; another is the eviction itself where the public vote for the housemate that they would like to see evicted from the set of housemates with the most nominations. The eviction process is a live show, the culmination of the week. Here is how the housemates reacted to the eviction of Spencer, who at the time was another very popular housemate.

Aftershock

The psychological reaction of the housemates on hearing of Spencer's eviction is one of complete surprise and intense shock. It's not dissimilar to the way that close relatives feel when they hear of someone's sudden death. His closest allies were literally shocked into a state of no response and were unable to console or comfort effectively in this initial period. It was eight seconds before anyone responded to the news and that was Tim's cursory touch. It was 20 seconds before PJ touched Spencer's shoulder and 4 minutes before Kate's first tentative touch. She then waited a full 15 minutes before actually hugging Spencer. Kate is unable to conceal the negative emotions that leak out through her facial expressions. These expressions are blends of fear, surprise and sadness. Her unconscious hand-to-head movements, known as self-adaptors, also reveal her need for some self-comfort. Her humming is an attempt to block out the reality of the current situation. It takes one and a half hours for her to let herself go completely with a show of tears.

   PJ's shock isn't just at the loss of a loved one but also a shock of the housemates' changed situation. By repeatedly congratulating Alex he is ingratiating himself with the new leader in the house. The fact that PJ also announces that he is looking for a new father figure underlies that he is not contending for the alpha-male role. He offers this role tentatively to Jonny, Alex and Tim in turn before explicitly directing this offer to Alex who rejects it. Spencer's shock eviction will lead to a period of rapid realignment in the *Big Brother* house. The housemates are desperate to come to terms with their new feelings of uncertainty. Many of them will now be feeling 'If Spencer can go any of us can'.

Psychologists had commented in the past on the uses of touch for comfort, but this incident shows us something about another dimension of touch – its timing. It shows that touch is not used immediately. There is a delay before it occurs. The incident also illustrates the use of self-touching as a comfort device. These aspects of behaviour become interesting and relevant because they help us interpret what has happened at a broader level in terms of the relationships in the group.

The *Big Brother* viewers, through time, become interested in the fortunes of individual housemates. Some of the psychology pieces reflected this interest. In the extract below I attempted to summarize Jonny's situation halfway through the series.

Joker wanted

At the halfway mark the housemate who's been most affected by the *Big Brother* experience is Jonny. He walked in as the self-proclaimed house joker and entertainer. Through a psychological process called self-verification Jonny invited the other housemates to accept a well-tested image, which formed the basis of his identity. From the beginning Jonny was one of the most visible housemates, but for most of the last four weeks and despite surviving this week's public vote, he's been withdrawn and at times virtually frozen, paralysed by his inability to make an impact on the group. He's become the invisible housemate. After week one Jonny suffered a series of severe blows. First there was Alison's eviction and then he was nominated himself in week two. In week three Sandy dealt the final blow to Jonny's sense of worth.

> SANDY: I actually didn't like you.

Six days later Jonny shaved his head, an act of huge symbolic significance as an attempt to shed his old self-image. The result is a man who displays a combination of behaviours sometimes found in depression. He sleeps till after midday, he's up alone at night and obsessively questions his own identity in the house. After being nominated for eviction for the second time Jonny thought he could become someone else.

But Jonny has a problem translating his wish into reality. Jonny's confidential chat with the *Big Brother* counsellor might have helped him realize even further that he must remain true to himself.

Now with the house changing as the second half of *Big Brother* gets underway, there is role for an entertainer.

> KATE: I can still say that my first week in the house was my best week, because I had such a good one, I'd never ever laughed so much in all my life.
> PJ: I just want a bit of fun back into this experience. It's not all doom and gloom, it shouldn't be.

If Jonny can claim back his old identity as house joker he might find himself in a very powerful position. If he fails to see that the role of joker is up for grabs he could condemn himself permanently to the role of invisible man.

Here we have a resumé piece summarizing the position of one character halfway through the experience, alerting the viewer as to what to look out for next, attempting to make sense of his psychological position in the house. The producers of the show encouraged the psychologists to produce psychology pieces that were predictive where possible. The pieces should allow the viewer to anticipate what might happen next if the observations and the interpretation were correct. In the Jonny piece there was a degree of prediction.

Relationships in the *Big Brother* house are always fascinating to the viewer. They may not be the relationships of great literature – in fact they are often quite ordinary, mundane affairs – but I suppose that is their real attraction. They are relationships like our own, relationships that we can identify with. We watch them build, sometimes very slowly, with this almost 360-degree perspective we have on them. Relationships caught from every angle night and day, in the presence of the other and in the absence of the other, and we try to make sense of the conflicting and difficult signals as best we can.

The odd couple

This year *Big Brother* has been strewn with budding relationships. Alex and Adele, Kate and Spencer, PJ and Jade, Lee and Sophie. But all came to nothing as they were mostly about power and protection. But there is one relationship in the house that might be genuine and that's Alex and Kate. Since they entered the *Big Brother* house, Kate and Alex have gone through an intense and at times stormy relationship with a surprising number of twists. The start was really promising, but on week two the situation had turned around completely. Kate and Spencer are playing with oranges. Alex confronts Kate about this.

ALEX: We've got to eat those fruit afterwards.

Alex reveals his feelings of jealousy whilst testing how Kate feels about him. The function of this argument is to separate Kate and Spencer and to turn Alex into the focus of Kate's attention. At the peak of the drama, Alex reveals his real thoughts with a striking example of a micro-expression. He smiles displaying a very brief look of real pleasure. The outcome of the argument is very satisfactory for Alex. The game between Kate and Spencer has been interrupted and Spencer now plays with Adele. Kate's anger demonstrates Alex's power to hurt her and therefore her unconscious emotional attachment to him. With Spencer and Adele out of the picture and with the house finally reunited, by the removal of the bars, Kate and Alex have become increasingly close. They display a lot of playful behaviours. The jacuzzi provides a real opportunity for intimacy to develop. There is a lot of touching as Kate washes Alex's back, but this is functional touching and there is very little bodily contact. There are signs of intimacy between them but these seem to be constrained by the invisible bubble which each of them has created around themselves. Neither of them wants to be the first to burst this bubble. Kate and Alex have been through a lot but now they are finally in a position to explore the depths of their feelings for each other, but they are afraid of each other's rejection. If Kate and Alex do survive in the house until the final week they might let their guard down and their up-and-down relationship would then be able to flourish at last.

Here we can see the significance of the micro-expression, that fleeting facial expression which leaks out very quickly to display the real emotion. Some might have picked up this micro-expression when it was played in real time but it has now been slowed down for all to see, and this micro-expression really holds the key to the previous set of behaviours. Suddenly we were living in a different world, where there is fast, fleeting action underpinning the routine, mundane aspects of everyday life; fast, fleeting action that may hold the key to what is going on.

Of course, there have been popular books in the past on 'body language', many of them extremely well known and popular, but they tended to focus on slow behaviours – posture and sometimes postural mirroring, interpersonal distance, levels of eye gaze. The books would discuss them as if the levels of each of these behaviours were fixed, rather than being the fast, dynamic behaviours that characterize everyday interaction. It is the changes in posture and brief periods of postural mirroring that often seem to be significant in everyday interaction. But how do we capture and describe these behaviours without the use of video-recording and without detailed slowed-down analyses? Body language books seem to be based on real-time observations, usually with drawings to illustrate the 'action', which is usually anything but. Such books sweep many of the important questions to one side. How long, for example, should two people mirror each other before it becomes significant? How do we know that the mirroring isn't simply due to chance? There are after all only a limited number of ways that people can sit on a settee. What about the temporary leanings to and leanings away that affect interpersonal distance? What about the patterns of eye gaze in which the individuals concerned sometimes make eye contact and sometimes do not? How do we identify the very brief facial expressions, the micro-expressions, which flit across the human face in interaction? What about the very quick movements of the hands and arms that appear to be rather closely linked to the content of the speech itself? These are the very behaviours that constitute everyday interaction and unfortunately most popular body language books do not have a lot to say about them. In these popular books, the behaviours tend to be slow and observable, indeed somewhat ponderous, and they always seem to be congruent with each other – high levels of eye contact and high levels of postural mirroring means 'liking'. But what about low levels of eye contact and high levels of postural mirroring at the same time? The pattern of behaviour is frozen in time and can therefore be portrayed in a still photograph or still drawing (if only people really stayed that still during real interaction) and the speech is almost always totally irrelevant. The speech is never transcribed in the images of the body language and the slow ponderous behaviours themselves are meant to tell us everything that we may ever need to know 'to penetrate the personal secrets of strangers, friends and lovers'. If only it were that easy.

As soon as people start moving, talking and displaying behaviours quite incongruent with each other, such 'penetration' becomes much more difficult and our analyses, unfortunately or fortunately depending on your point of view, have to become that much more sophisticated. It is also important to remind ourselves that these popular body language books are often 30 years out of date with respect to the relevant psychological literature. In this book I will attempt to integrate the latest thinking in psychological research with this new archive of material from *Big Brother* to offer a new account of certain dynamic aspects of body language (certain aspects only because even here the story starts to get very complicated) and how these work alongside ordinary verbal language in everyday social interaction. I will not be arguing that popular body language books overestimated the importance of the nonverbal aspects of communication, far from it, but their theoretical accounts and interpretations often quite simply missed the point.

To return to the *Big Brother* material, it is important to point out that psychologists have in the past had detailed footage of human behaviour, but this was often of psychology students themselves in the laboratory, most often recorded in experimental situations. None was quite as rich as *Big Brother* and very often it was not even natural; it was merely students carrying out a variety of artificial experimental tasks with little meaning to them. Oxford undergraduates, complete strangers to one another, were asked 'to get to know each other in the laboratory'. 'Why?' 'What are you studying?' 'What are you trying to discover?' I wasn't there, but I can almost certainly hear some of these questions being asked. Sheffield students were simply asked to have a conversation 'as naturally as possible' in front of the one-way mirror. 'How exactly?' 'What sort of conversation?' 'What are we allowed to talk about?' 'For what purpose?' 'When do we know when to stop?' I was there this time and heard some of these questions as participants were guided into a cold, soulless room and instructed to remove their coats (if at all possible) before beginning their 'natural' conversation. The resultant behaviours probably reflected in quite deep and mysterious ways some of these underlying concerns.

As a PhD student at Cambridge interested in the dynamics of social interaction I put great emphasis on natural behaviour in my own research, where natural meant behaviour that would be occurring anyway and not just because I wanted it to happen at the time I wanted it to happen. After some thought, I ended up video-recording the kinds of natural behaviour, indeed the only kinds, that I could think of which occur naturally in psychology departments – I recorded academic discussions, tutorials, supervisions and seminars on psychology topics. I must confess that I knew little about the students and the academics except what they displayed in their tutorial hour, nervous to the end in front of the hidden cameras (this research is summarized in Beattie 1983).

In *Big Brother*, on the other hand, we do know something about who these people are in front of the camera. They are there for weeks on end and their self-consciousness may never quite disappear but it surely fades, more than in the case of the participants in other psychological research who are never there long enough to allow this to happen. *Big Brother* constitutes a rich source of material of multi-layered social interaction: we have fierce abrupt arguments and long sessions of bonding; we find flirtation and the evasion of the morning after; we see alliances forming and coming apart; and we can see the levels and layers in all of this. We see groups of people living in front of the cameras hour after hour, day after day. In this book I will use examples from *Big Brother* to argue for a new conception as to how to think about human social behaviour and in particular as to how to think about nonverbal communication. The new ideas do not come from the show but some of the best examples of the behaviours that I am interested in do, and these examples are critical to the ideas that I wish to get across here.

As a *Big Brother* psychologist my area of specialization is the bodily communication of the contestants: their body language, their facial expressions including the micro-expressions, the silent signals of the eyes, head nods, postural changes and the mirroring of posture, hand movements, interpersonal distance, winks, fidgeting and eyebrow raising. Some of these we see quite clearly and some seem to pass us by quickly and unnoticed both in real life and on the television screen, except when they are pointed out to us.

In the first *Big Brother* series I described how Mel's behaviour changed when the attractive stranger Claire was introduced to the house, after the eviction of Nasty Nick. I described how Mel's posture changed and how she took up a closed bodily position as an unconscious response to

Claire's introduction to the house. I suggested what that might mean about her underlying attitude to Claire (it was classic popular 'body language' stuff, the relatively enduring postural change easy to identify even by relatively unobservant viewers). I detected early signs of Mel and Andy's mutual attraction through synchrony in the timing of their bodily movements, their interactional synchrony. I described how the degree of interactional synchrony changed through time.

In the second series I described Stuart's very visible winking behaviour and how he used it to build alliances within the house, although the immortal line 'Stuart is the biggest winker in the house' was left to my colleague, the Oxford psychologist Peter Collett. My theme here was how Stuart used winking as a covert strategy for establishing control in the group, but I pointed out the dangers in employing such a strategy because although the wink placed Stuart firmly in control, there was something of a dangerous paradox at play here. I said: 'Whilst Stuart is in control, that wink is accepted and taken at face value. But should any mistrust of his motives creep in, that wink will seem to have a rather different value, and will be seen as him being two-faced. It could easily backfire on him.' Winking was always going to be a dangerous strategy for Stuart, and so it turned out. He was the second housemate to be evicted from the *Big Brother* house in the second series.

In that same series, I analysed the facial expressions of the contestants and searched for the presence of micro-expressions, fully formed expressions of emotion which usually last for less than a quarter of a second and can reveal the contestants' true emotional state. We normally miss these in everyday life, but in the world of *Big Brother* we can see them quite clearly when they are played in slow motion for us. Who can forget Helen's facial expression when she asked Josh which of the female housemates he would choose to sleep with? 'Who would you sleep with?' she asked. A question she then repeated for good measure and when he replied 'Amma' her fleeting micro-expression spoke volumes.

I also searched for squelched emotions, where an emotion starts to form on the face but the individual realizes what is happening and manages to suppress the expression, usually with a smile – the smile being the great cover-up expression, used to hide a whole range of negative emotions. I analysed all of the smiles of the contestants at various stages of the contest and differentiated between genuine and false smiles. Voluntary or deliberate facial movements, like false smiles, are controlled by the cerebral hemispheres and show an asymmetry in their expression on the face as a result of this. Involuntary facial movements that reflect real emotion, such as genuine smiles, are controlled by lower, more primitive areas of the brain and are essentially symmetrical on both sides of the face. I also pointed out the characteristic way in which false smiles leave the face, either leaving much too abruptly or much too slowly, quite unlike real smiles in this regard. Real smiles also involve the muscles around the eyes in ways that false smiles do not. I pointed out that it is much easier to fake a false smile around the mouth region than around the eyes (see Ekman 1985; Lee and Beattie 1998).

My analysis here revealed that during the first 24 hours in the *Big Brother* house, the most common facial expression of the new contestants was the smile. At the time, I said:

Smiles are very effective social signals. By smiling a lot, the housemates are trying to create as favourable an impression as possible, and to form bonds with others but the smile is also one of the most common masks people use in everyday interaction. It can reflect positive emotions, like happiness, but it can also be used to cover more negative ones. When the housemates first met, many of their smiles covered initial responses to each other and their environment. They were false smiles, what we commonly call nervous smiles. We can distinguish real smiles from false smiles on the basis of a number of behavioural cues . . . in the first half an hour in the house, two-thirds of all smiles were false smiles. As the housemates become more familiar with each other, the smile remains the dominant expression, but it doesn't mean that people are entirely comfortable with each other. Some housemates have quite specific strategies of smiling. These smiling strategies may have an important role to play in the weeks to come.

It was interesting that when I was looking for examples of asymmetric false smiles from the first few days in the house to illustrate the point, given the time pressure involved, the best examples all seemed to come from Elizabeth. I pointed this out to my producer, Rachel Barnes. 'Only one example of a false smile from any one contestant,' she warned, in case it might be thought that I was saying that Elizabeth's smiles were particularly false at the very start of the show. I might have influenced the pattern of voting through the selection of my examples. This after all was a television programme with winners and losers.

I analysed the smiles and facial expressions of the contestants and noted who mirrored whose posture and which members of the house displayed perfect synchrony in movement during their conversations, and which did not. Each week I presented a series of interpretations of what was happening in the *Big Brother* house and a number of hypotheses as to what was going to happen next. The viewers seemed to enjoy these psychological analyses because in the second and third series the 'psychology show' became the most popular show after the live eviction show. We were all psychologists now, interested in the fine detail of human behaviour because it might help us to understand the stories unfolding in front of us.

In the third series I presented for the first time some new ideas about bodily communication. I spent a lot of time analysing the hand movements of the housemates in painstaking detail and offered a number of hypotheses about how these movements reflected the housemates' underlying thinking. But why was I focusing so much on the movements of the hands? What can the hands really tell us? What can any aspect of bodily communication tell us about thinking? Surely it's all about emotion and interpersonal relationships? This is what this book is all about. It outlines a new theory of one aspect of bodily communication, namely the movement of the hands and arms as people speak. The theory holds that the hands represent the human mind in action. They provide us with a window on the human mind, where we can glimpse some of the unarticulated thinking that goes along with speech. I will explain how the ideas developed and outline some of the philosophical and practical implications of this new theory. Behaviour in the *Big Brother* house will provide many of the examples for analysis. But if you have never seen *Big Brother*, and have absolutely no wish ever to watch it, the examples and the argument should still make considerable sense to you.

Two separate languages? 2

The focus on nonverbal behaviour, (bodily communication and some vocal aspects of speech), as the significant domain through which human emotion is expressed, relationships are built and interpersonal attitudes are negotiated and expressed, has a long and distinguished history in psychology and in related disciplines. The argument has always been that language, the verbal channel of communication, is used primarily to convey factual or semantic information about the world, whereas the nonverbal channels have primarily social functions – 'to manage the immediate social relationships – as in animals', according to Oxford psychologist Michael Argyle, writing in 1972.

This functional separation of language and nonverbal behaviour is something of an established orthodoxy in psychology. Again the psychologist Michael Argyle, this time writing with clinical psychologist Peter Trower in 1979, states: 'Humans use two quite separate languages [language and nonverbal communication], each with its own function.' This is perhaps the most basic and therefore the clearest statement of how psychologists view language and non-verbal communication and their relationship. In a similar vein, Peter Trower, Bridget Bryant and Michael Argyle in their book *Social Skills and Mental Health* (1978) write: 'In human social behaviour it looks as if the nonverbal channel is used for negotiating interpersonal attitudes while the verbal channel is used primarily for conveying information.'

Language has always been considered to be linked to thought and to communicate information about the world. 'It will rain tomorrow in Manchester, again', is easily conveyed by language, but not at all easily conveyed by nonverbal communication. I have just tried to do this consciously and believe me it is very difficult. It is 'Manchester' that I just can't do and I have a bit of trouble with 'again' (and with 'tomorrow', if I'm being totally honest), although 'rain' is more or less alright (my fingers pitter-patter downwards). Nonverbal communication, it is argued, does other sorts of things than convey information about the world and the weather in Manchester. It conveys information about our emotional state, about whether we like someone or not, about whose turn it is in social interaction. It is verbal language that distinguishes us from other animals (as well as 'drinking when we are not thirsty and making love all year round', as Pierre-Augustin Caron de Beaumarchais notes in *The Marriage of Figaro*); it is nonverbal communication that we share with other animals.

Charles Hockett writing in 1960 identified 13 design features that all human verbal languages possess to convey information about the external environment (and about everything else as well). I will identify some of the most significant here. All languages use the vocal–auditory channel and, given the physics of sound, a linguistic signal can be heard by any auditory system within earshot and the source localized by any hearer, and there is rapid fading of the signal. This has potentially important implications in terms of evolutionary pressures:

> The rapid fading of such a signal means that it does not linger for reception at the hearer's convenience. Animal tracks and spoors, on the other hand, persist for a while; so of course do written records, a product of man's extremely recent cultural evolution.
>
> (Hockett 1960: 90)

In any communicative system the relationship between meaningful messages and their meanings can be either arbitrary or non-arbitrary. In verbal language this relationship is arbitrary, as Hockett writes:

'Salt' is not salty or granular. 'Whale' is a small word for a large object; 'microorganism' is the reverse. A picture, on the other hand, looks like what it is a picture of. A bee dances faster if the source of the nectar she is reporting is closer, and slower if it is farther away. The design feature of 'arbitrariness' has the disadvantage of being arbitrary, but the great advantage that there is no limit to what can be communicated about.

(Hockett 1960: 90)

Human language can also be used to talk about things that are remote in space and time (the design feature of 'displacement') and it is an open system. We can convey an infinite number of messages using a finite number of words or morphemes, applying a set of rules or principles (the design feature of 'productivity'). Wilhelm von Humboldt's famous dictum was that language provides a finite means for generating an infinite variety of expressive forms. In other words, human language is a very powerful system of communication, which is infinitely flexible and yet immediately comprehensible to all who understand the language.

So verbal language has a number of distinctive characteristics. Nonverbal communication is considered to be quite different to this, different in design and different in function. The traditional view of the function of nonverbal communication is that it does not communicate semantic information about the (inner or outer) world but signals emotional state and attitudes crucial to the forming and development of interpersonal relationships. Of course, this position intuitively makes some sort of sense. One advantage of interpersonal matters being dealt with nonverbally, as psychologists have noted, is that the expression of such attitudes can be kept vague and flexible. Again, according to Michael Argyle (1972): 'People need not reveal clearly nor commit themselves to what they think about each other.' Once we start using language to communicate our attitudes to another person, then everything is out in the open in quite a different way. We are publicly committed to what we have said and therefore accountable. 'You said that you loved me' is a perfectly reasonable retort. 'You acted like you loved me, there was just something momentary in your facial expression and in your eyes' is much weaker somehow. But that is just one aspect of the process. The anthropologist Gregory Bateson highlights another important aspect:

> It seems that the discourse of nonverbal communication is precisely concerned with matters of relationship . . . From an adaptive point of view, it is therefore important that this discourse be carried on by techniques which are relatively unconscious and only imperfectly subject to voluntary control.
>
> (Bateson 1968: 614–15)

We can all say 'I love you', some rather too easily. It is quite a different matter to fake love nonverbally, or so Gregory Bateson seems to think. So the argument goes that we express relationships nonverbally because these types of communication are less subject to voluntary control, and therefore presumably more honest, and yet at the same time are more nebulous. We send out signals and yet remain unaccountable for their expression.

These views about the separate functions of language and nonverbal communication are not confined to psychology, as we have already seen. Gregory Bateson also states that 'nonverbal communication serves functions totally different from those of language and performs functions that verbal language is unsuited to perform'. He continues that 'nonverbal communication is precisely concerned with matters of relationship – love, hate, respect, fear, dependency, etc. – between self and vis-à-vis or between self and environment'. He was also concerned with conflicts between these two channels, when the verbal channel says one thing directly but the nonverbal channel says something completely different, and the effects of such conflicts on others. He introduced the concept of the 'double bind' as an aberrant form of self-contradictory communication, which may play a pivotal role in the development of schizophrenia within families, particularly in communication from the mother to the child (an idea taken up by the British psychiatrist R. D. Laing 1964, and others). The problem with 'double binds' is that there is no rational response permitted to such contradictory communications.

The argument therefore within psychology and other disciplines has been that nonverbal communication performs functions that language is unsuitable to perform and that verbal language, on the other hand, that peculiarly human attribute, is concerned with the world of thinking and abstract ideas and the communication of complex information about the world. It makes perfect sense therefore for a psychologist interested in relationships and emotions in the *Big Brother* house to concentrate more or less exclusively on nonverbal communication. I say 'more or less' because on occasion from the second series I did analyse the verbal and nonverbal strategies of individuals in the house. For example, the extract below shows how I described the behaviour of Stuart in the first week in the house in the second series. I focused on both his nonverbal behaviour, including his spatial behaviour and its effects on eye contact, and his verbal behaviour, including the pattern of turn taking.

As the group settles into this week's task, Stuart settles into his role here. Stuart was called to the Diary Room to be given the instructions, and thus has an arbitrary advantage, which he capitalizes on. He strategically arranges the group in a large arc around him so that he can maintain eye contact with each and every member, but they can't maintain eye contact with those immediately adjacent to them. Think of a conductor in an orchestra: this is how he has positioned himself, and it gives him an enormous advantage in controlling the flow of conversation. The effectiveness of this can be seen in the fact that the rest of the group restrict their responses to appropriate junctures in his speech – they do not overlap with his talk. It's as if he was directing them to respond only in certain places, like a conductor telling musicians when to play. After he gets to the end of the instructions, there is genuine and widespread competition for the floor. Stuart leaves them to it: he doesn't want to compete on level terms. However, eventually a suggestion is made that he likes, and he allows that view to be spread among the group. The motion is carried, but see whose hand goes up first [Stuart's], indicating this is a particular view he agrees with. He has controlled the whole sequence, but not appeared to be overbearing. He knows when to step back and let others fight it out.

If we are thinking about issues of power and control, especially with regard to the organization of turn taking in a discussion, then it seems obvious to consider both verbal and nonverbal behaviour, but at other times when we are analysing behaviour it seems natural and equally obvious to focus on either language or nonverbal behaviour, on the assumption that they are quite separate and that people use them for quite different functions. If you are interested in the communication of complex ideas you study language; if you are interested in emotion and relationships you study nonverbal behaviour. That is the established orthodoxy, an orthodoxy which was reflected in the tasks assigned to the psychologists working on *Big Brother*.

But what happens if this orthodoxy is wrong? Where does that leave us? What happens if people use verbal language as much as nonverbal behaviour for the subtle communication of their attitudes towards each other? What happens, and this idea does seem strange, if nonverbal behaviour is used instead of, or alongside, language, for the communication of complex ideas? What happens if we do use nonverbal behaviour to communicate ideas like 'it will rain tomorrow in Manchester, again', despite my conscious efforts a few pages earlier, which failed miserably? And let me be clear here. I'm not talking about sign language like British Sign Language or American Sign Language for the deaf, which are types of verbal language anyway with a dictionary and a syntax or set of rules for combining the individual words. They are types of verbal language transmitted using the body rather than the voice (although, of course, they do not have Hockett's design feature of use of the vocal–auditory channel, but they do have the critical design features of 'arbitrariness', 'displacement' and 'productivity' among others).

I'm talking about nonverbal behaviour as we usually think of it – behaviour acquired through the normal processes of socialization, without the acquisition of a dictionary of items and syntax for combining them into meaningful sentences. I'm talking about nonverbal behaviour where meaning can be transmitted in a more global and spontaneous fashion than this. I'm talking about a new idea that has arisen principally as a consequence of the work of an American psychologist called David McNeill (1985, 1992) who has produced a new theory of how the mind works (but see also Adam Kendon's extremely important work 1972, 1980, 1988). This is the idea I will be exploring in this book. I will outline McNeill's theory and discuss my own research in this particular area. These ideas challenge the established orthodoxy in psychology and they have potentially enormous theoretical and practical implications for gaining a much greater insight into what people are really thinking as they talk.

I will argue that language and some nonverbal behaviour are not separate in the way that most psychologists have thought. They are not separate in terms of how they are produced and they are not separate in terms of what they do. My first shot across the bows of this established orthodoxy will involve reconsidering some classic research in psychology, which purports to show that when language and nonverbal communication are both used explicitly to communicate interpersonal attitudes, the language channel is virtually ignored. The claim is that language plays virtually no role in such matters. This is reflected in widely known and widely quoted statements of the kind that when it comes to the social world and interpersonal relations 'only 7 per cent of communication is verbal'. Forget verbal language, it says, concentrate exclusively on the nonverbal bit. The problem is that the research from which this conclusion derives is really quite weak. We turn first to consider the possible limitations of the classic psychological experiments from which this apparent conclusion is derived.

There are two sets of critical experiments that are crucial here. The first set was carried out by Albert Mehrabian at the University of California in Los Angeles and published in a number of important studies in the late 1960s (Mehrabian and Ferris 1967; Mehrabian and Wiener 1967). Mehrabian investigated the effects of consistencies and inconsistencies in communication between the various channels of communication, including the actual meaning of the words and the tone of voice in which they are spoken and the facial expressions and the tone of voice, on the communication of interpersonal attitudes, and in particular on judgements of degrees of liking. In the first study he selected three words judged to convey liking – 'honey', 'thanks' and 'dear'; three words judged to be neutral in this regard – 'maybe', 'really' and 'oh'; and three words that conveyed dislike – 'don't', 'brute' and 'terrible'. Two female speakers read each of the nine selected words using positive, neutral and negative vocal expressions and these communications were then played to sets of judges. In a second study, one neutral word was selected, the word 'maybe'. This time the facial expression was varied: it was positive, neutral or negative. Judges in this second study were presented with an audio recording of the message and a photograph of the person delivering the message. The judges had to rate the overall communication to determine how positive or negative it came across.

From these studies Mehrabian concluded that in the communication of interpersonal attitudes the facial and the vocal channels greatly outweigh the verbal channel and he estimated the relative contributions of the three channels as 55 per cent for the facial channel, 38 per cent for the vocal channel and 7 per cent for the verbal channel. Mehrabian's conclusion was 'when there is inconsistency between verbally and implicitly expressed attitude, the implicit proportion [the nonverbal component] will dominate in determining the total message'.

This is the first study that attempted to say exactly how much the verbal and nonverbal channels each contribute to the communication of interpersonal attitudes and it produced a set of figures that have been picked up and adopted within popular culture. Most of us have heard things such as nonverbal behaviour is 13 times more powerful than language in the expression of interpersonal attitudes, and that facial expression is 8 times more powerful than language. If you read almost any copy of *Cosmopolitan* magazine you will see these figures quoted not just by journalists but also by experts, including psychologists. A contemporary advert for a credit card begins with the statement that 'only 7 per cent of communication is verbal', which is exactly Mehrabian's estimate, so the advert continues 'make the other 93 per cent count', presumably by using this particular credit card, which is meant to say a lot about you.

But the problem with these psychological studies is that they don't really consider language at all in the expression of interpersonal attitudes; at least not language as we normally understand it with meaningful sentences used to express how we feel. Only individual words, like 'honey', 'brute' and 'maybe' were used. Nobody talks in individual words in the real world for prolonged periods of time, when they can help it. 'Honey' as an expression on its own only gets you so far. Then when Mehrabian considered the effects of facial versus vocal cues, these different cues were not presented together on videotape but merely as a photograph accompanying a single word. In other words, the participants in this study were simply presented with a photograph of a particular facial expression and they heard the single word being said and then they had to integrate these two things in their mind and make their judgement. So this experiment made no real attempt to simulate anything approaching normal social behaviour or normal social judgement. Hence, we have to be a little wary about the conclusions that have been drawn from it.

However, two experiments carried out a bit later at Oxford in the early 1970s by Michael Argyle and his colleagues seem at first sight to address many of these issues. The experiments were published as two important studies, indeed 'citation classics', by Argyle, Salter, Nicholson,

Williams, and Burgess (1970) and by Argyle, Alkema and Gilmour (1971). For a long period of time before his death in 2002, Argyle was a leading British social psychologist, perhaps the leading British social psychologist, one of the pioneers of the experimental study of human nonverbal behaviour using a series of often ingenious experiments. His goal was to lay bare the very basis of our everyday behaviour, as well as among other things attempting to assess what makes people happy using detailed psychological analyses. He was famous at a more personal level for his dry sense of humour, his lifelong interest in Scottish country dancing and his slightly unusual style of social interaction, which made some comment that he was indeed researching something that many, perhaps including himself, found difficult and problematic – social behaviour with all of its layers and hidden depths.

The basic methodology of these experiments is quite ingenious but it does require careful scrutiny. Very briefly, three verbal messages, paragraphs this time rather than individual words (hostile, neutral or friendly in one experiment; superior, neutral or inferior in another), were delivered in each of three different nonverbal styles (the friendly style being 'warm, soft tone of voice, open posture, smiling face', the hostile style being 'harsh voice, closed posture, frown with teeth showing'). Care was taken at the outset to ensure that the verbal message and the nonverbal style had approximately the same effects on listener evaluation on certain specific dimensions. Here is an example of the types of message used in this experiment. This is the hostile message: 'I don't much enjoy meeting the subjects who take part in these experiments. I often find them rather boring and difficult to deal with. Please don't hang around too long afterwards and talk about the experiment. Some people who come as subjects are really rather disagreeable.'

The combined communications, with the three verbal messages delivered in each of the three verbal styles, were then rated by judges to see how friendly or hostile the resultant messages were perceived as being. The results again apparently demonstrate quite clearly that the nonverbal channel greatly outweighs the verbal channel in the communication of interpersonal attitudes. For example, on a seven-point scale, where '7' means extremely friendly and '1' means extremely hostile, the hostile verbal message delivered in a friendly nonverbal style was rated as 5.17; in other words it was perceived as being towards the friendly end of the scale and higher than the mid-point of 4. When the nonverbal style was friendly it didn't really seem to matter what was actually said; the overall communication was perceived as friendly. Similarly, when the nonverbal style was hostile, again it didn't really seem to matter what was said. The difference in perception of the friendly and hostile verbal messages delivered in the hostile nonverbal style was trivial, the scores being 1.60 and 1.80 respectively. Indeed the hostile verbal message delivered in the hostile style was perceived as slightly friendlier than the friendly message in the hostile style. This latter form of communication is, of course, essentially a conflicting communication of the type Bateson termed a 'double bind'.

These results led Michael Argyle to the conclusion that nonverbal communication is twelve and a half times more powerful than language in the communication of interpersonal attitudes, specifically on the friendliness–hostility dimension, and over ten times more powerful in the communication of a different interpersonal attitude, namely superiority–inferiority.

These figures are very similar to those of Mehrabian and have become an important part of our everyday culture. This series of studies obviously struck a chord with the public and gave those who wished to discuss the importance of nonverbal communication precise figures to work with. The studies demonstrate that nonverbal communication is not just highly significant, but also that we can virtually dismiss verbal language if we want to understand how interpersonal attitudes are signalled, and interpersonal relations are built, in everyday life. It also means that we can ignore the connections between language and nonverbal communication because the judges in this experiment seem to do just that. Much is built on these two sets of studies. But in my view these pioneering and very influential studies have fundamental weaknesses that really do limit the conclusions that can be drawn. Let's consider what these might be.

The Oxford studies involve judges having to watch a set of nine successive communications on videotape, all from the same person, tapes in which the language and nonverbal communication are systematically varied. Therefore the whole point of the experiment would be immediately obvious to anyone who took part. Participants could quickly work out what the experimenter was getting at and therefore might decide to play along with him or her. This sometimes happens in psychological research and is called the 'demand characteristics' of the experiment. (Sometimes the opposite occurs: the participants work out what the experimenter wants and deliberately do not go along with it. This is known rather more colloquially as the 'f... you' effect.) This is always a problem for psychological research where the point of the experiment is as obvious as it was here.

Second, in order to try to measure the relative importance of language and nonverbal communication, the strength of the two channels had to be both measured and equated at the outset. They had to be equal in strength when measured independently. These studies therefore, at best, tell us about people's perceptions of a certain class of communication with the range of the strength of the components artificially set. The studies do not tell us anything about the range of effects produced by language and nonverbal communication in the world at large. Perhaps in the real world people do not use such explicitly friendly or unfriendly messages. Consider that hostile verbal statement again: 'I don't much enjoy meeting the subjects who take part in these experiments. I often find them rather boring and difficult to deal with.' Is that ever likely to be said directly to someone apart from as a joke? And when it is accompanied by a friendly verbal style ('warm, soft tone of voice, smile, open posture') how else is this supposed to be understood apart from as some sort of joke with the verbal statement to be dismissed? Don't forget that this is exactly what was found to happen in this experiment.

What would happen if we did not make the message quite as explicit as this? What would happen if we made the verbal message slightly more real and then used the same basic pattern of delivery? How would it then be perceived? Would the nonverbal component still make the verbal component seem completely unimportant? Let's do a quick mind experiment. Let's start with something pretty explicit but (in my experience) quite plausible: 'Would you mind leaving?'.

This is delivered in the:

1. friendly nonverbal style 'warm, soft tone of voice, open posture, smiling face'

or in the:

2. hostile nonverbal style 'harsh voice, closed posture, frown with teeth showing'.

You have to imagine both. Perhaps you could try delivering both messages in front of a mirror, or better still try delivering them to a friend. I am afraid that in both cases I think that I would get the message and go. The first message I imagine being delivered by 'the hostess with the mostest', you know the kind of person I mean. She is asking me to leave a posh party. The second I imagine being delivered by a nightclub bouncer. Both are clearly hostile but 'the hostess with the mostest', whilst hostile, is keeping it under control mainly for the benefit of the other guests (hence the friendly nonverbal style). The verbal message is, however, significantly more important in communicating her basic unfriendly attitude here than any accompanying behaviours. It may be explicit but it is a real request, heard many times, I would imagine, at many dinner parties (or is this just me?).

Or what about something that is a statement rather than a request or a command, something as basic as: 'You used to be such a nice person'?

Again this is delivered in the:

3. friendly nonverbal style 'warm, soft tone of voice, open posture, smiling face'

or in the:

4. hostile nonverbal style 'harsh voice, closed posture, frown with teeth showing'.

My guess is that the nonverbal behaviour in message 3 will neither transform nor soften the basic message. It is not a friendly statement and the fact that it is being delivered in this style could make it even less friendly because it is as if the speaker is still trying to be understanding yet despite being understanding she can still make the basic statement. In message 4 the person has started to lose control.

The point to be made here is that psychologists have never really been able to quantify the relative importance of language and nonverbal communication in interpersonal communication. It would be an extremely difficult and time-consuming experiment to do. I have made it seem easy with a few examples, but think of the generality of the conclusions that people are trying to draw from such an experiment. We would need a representative sample of an enormous variety of utterances, sampling all of the kinds of things that language can do and sampling different contexts as well. I have sketched in a few contexts above, but I am sure you can imagine some different contexts that might affect the basic interpretation of the utterances. Utterances after all only make sense in context.

If you don't believe me let's return to the first utterance, this time imagining slightly different contexts for the utterance: 'Would you mind leaving?'.

Imagine this being delivered at the very end of the evening by a bouncer in a nightclub and delivered in that friendly style 'warm, soft tone of voice, open posture, smiling face'. Suddenly it's quite friendly. Everyone has to leave, it's just that time of night. The bouncer is, after all, asking in a very friendly manner. I tried this experiment, believe it or not. I asked a doorman I knew to ask people to leave using this style of nonverbal behaviour. I then asked the poor innocent punter how he perceived the message. At the end of the night the punter said: 'Everything was fine, the bouncer was polite and friendly. Are you doing some research into customer satisfaction?' I also asked the doorman to say exactly the same thing in the same friendly manner early in the evening to a different punter. This second punter looked confused. He thought that it was a case of mistaken identity; bouncers don't just ask you to leave for no good reason. But how did the new punter perceive the overall message – the 'hostile' message in the 'friendly' style (at this point I really do need to rely on inverted commas)? Actually, he perceived it as very threatening. 'It was the understated way that he asked me,' the second punter explained. 'He was really hostile, as if he was looking forward to giving me a good thump if I didn't go immediately. But I hadn't done anything,' he added, 'that was really the annoying thing.' He smiled when he was told that this was just a little test.

The picture is, as you can see, becoming a little more complicated. The conclusions, which are that interpersonal attitudes are signalled almost exclusively by nonverbal behaviour, are looking a little more shaky. The general conclusion that 'humans use two quite separate languages, each with its own function' is looking somewhat less secure.

But to return to the studies of Michael Argyle, how could we make them more convincing? As a starting point we would want to make sure that the behaviours studied in the laboratory mirrored the kinds of behaviours shown in the real world. We can all be hostile using language without being quite as explicit as the speaker was in these experiments. When verbal statements become less explicit and more plausible, and more like the things that are said in everyday life, do they then become more powerful and significant as a consequence, and not so readily dismissed as some sort of joke in an experiment of this kind? The important point is that we do not know because unfortunately this experiment has never been carried out.

At this point you might be wondering how verbal language would function to signal friendliness in subtle and less direct ways in everyday life. (I came up with a couple of quite hostile utterances off the top of my head, again I wonder what this tells you about me.) Here are a few suggestions. You can perhaps add your own here because the range of ways verbal language might do this is potentially quite large. But I would suggest that opening up a conversation in the first place, the use of first names, compliments, disclosure, reciprocated disclosure, the asking of personal questions, verbal engagement, shared perspectives, sharing of childhood memories, offers of help, offers of support, all play some role in the communication of certain interpersonal attitudes by language itself.

How important are each of these verbal strategies compared with the appropriate forms of nonverbal communication like facial expressions, postures, smiles and frowns in the overall communication of interpersonal attitudes? We simply do not know, but my guess is that the verbal statements would not be dismissed quite so readily as they were in those pioneering but somewhat transparent experiments of the early 1970s. Again this is not to argue against the incredible significance of nonverbal communication, but merely represents an attempt to reinstate ordinary language and the connections between ordinary language and nonverbal communication in the heart of social relationships and the study of human communication.

Let me also add that there are other rather more specific criticisms of these studies that are necessary given the incredible cultural weight which has come to rest on their conclusions. Only one person was used in these Oxford experiments to deliver the nine messages in the first place and she was described as 'an attractive female student'. In other words we know nothing about the generality of the results. How do we know that the results were not specific to this one individual? Would the results have generalized to male students, to less attractive students, or to the population at large? We don't know. But a number of years ago I tried to replicate the original study using a male speaker, and the results were altogether a good deal less clear-cut. For example, the friendly verbal message in a hostile nonverbal style was rated as 3.90, essentially perceived as neutral rather than as very hostile, as in the original study (see Beattie 1983: 9).

There is another very important point to make. In the original study the judges were watching the combinations of verbal and nonverbal communication on a video screen and were specifically requested to attend to the video clips. In real life, however, when we are engaged in social interaction we sometimes look at the other person, sometimes we do not. This shifting pattern of eye gaze depends upon interpersonal distance, relative status, seating or standing position, the content of what we are saying, the structure of what we are saying and emotions like shame, embarrassment, guilt, etc. In real life we may miss a number of critical nonverbal signals for a variety of reasons. In the classic experiments by Michael Argyle there was never this possibility. Again, these experiments failed to simulate the complexities and patterns of everyday social life. For this and for the other reasons outlined we need to be extremely careful about how we interpret the results of these classic experiments.

There are a number of lessons to be learnt here. We live in a world where body language is now understood to be of extraordinary importance in everyday social life and shows like *Big Brother* have made it seem even more significant. We are all becoming that bit more aware of the layers and complexities of human communication, including the nonverbal aspects of the whole process. This, of course, I approve of, but popular shows and popular books always work somehow within the established orthodoxy. When it comes to human communication, unfortunately or fortunately depending upon your point of view, the established orthodoxy may now need to be challenged. The claim that 'humans use two quite separate languages, each with its own function' may simply not be correct. First, the two languages may not be in any sense really separate, indeed I will argue in this book that they may be part of the same basic process. Second, language is almost certainly crucial to the communication of interpersonal attitudes, and classic experimental studies which suggest otherwise are themselves fundamentally flawed. Third and perhaps most important of all, the assumption that language functions to express thinking and abstract ideas and that nonverbal communication does not, and indeed cannot be used for this sort of thing, may also be incorrect. The old adage that no animal, armed only with nonverbal communication, could ever hope to express the idea that his or her family was poor but honest may have to be reconsidered in the light of the most recent theoretical research in psychology. This is what I am going to explore in this book.

I have always justified my involvement in *Big Brother* by arguing that we are all intuitive psychologists, interested in observing and interpreting the behaviour of the people around us. I have always thought that part of my job in *Big Brother* was to assist people in this process. But it seems to me that we also have to become psychologists in quite a different sense. We all have to learn to evaluate the evidence on which many psychological claims are based. We can see the shortcomings of the classic studies by Albert Mehrabian and Michael Argyle when we have some of the details in front of us. In this book I want to challenge the established orthodoxy on the functional separation of language and nonverbal communication and I want you, the reader, to understand the strength of the evidence. I want to challenge the very notion that some nonverbal behaviour is in any sense separate from language – the nonverbal behaviour in question being hand movements or gesture. I want to suggest instead, following the pioneering work of Adam Kendon and David McNeill, that gestures are closely linked to speech and 'yet present meaning in a form fundamentally different from that of speech' and that through hand movements 'people unwittingly display their inner thoughts and ways of understanding events of the world'. I want to argue that gestures open up a new way of regarding thinking and speech and the connections between them.

Such gestures can be a window on the human mind and allow us to see thoughts and images that would otherwise be quite invisible. This is new research in psychology and perhaps I should mention that I did make a plea each week to be allowed to bring some of these new insights into the analysis of human behaviour to bear on the show. The producers of the first two series were intrigued by my suggestions, but argued that it would require too much by way of introduction to have such ideas readily accepted. They relented in the third series and in *Celebrity Big Brother* in 2002. But these were still new ideas that would have to be introduced and developed. That is why I am writing this book – to introduce these new ideas so that in future programmes on the analysis of human behaviour we can all hopefully see that much more.

Let me end this chapter with a word of caution. I am an experimental psychologist. I don't want you just to accept the ideas that I am going to present here as a new orthodoxy. I don't want these new ideas to go unchallenged. I want you to understand where the ideas come from. The experiments from which the ideas derive are all very simple. They can be followed and understood by individuals with no background in psychology; an interest in understanding human social behaviour will suffice. But I think that it is worth learning about some of this research because in my opinion the new ideas that emerge from it may change forever how you think about human behaviour in general, and nonverbal communication in particular. You may also learn to read minds in a very real and in a very scientific sense.

Where the action is 3

The form of nonverbal behaviour that I will be focusing on in this book is movement of the hands and arms. Psychologists call these hand and arm movements 'gestures'. 'Gestures' is really quite a confusing term here because when we think of gestures we think of things like the palm-front V sign for peace or victory, or the palm-back V sign, the so-called 'Harvey Smith', which has quite a different meaning in the UK. These very special types of gesture are called 'emblems'. They substitute for words and are defined as gestures with a direct verbal translation. The palm-front V sign means peace or victory; the palm-back V sign means . . . well, you can translate the Harvey Smith for yourself. Emblems are gestures that are consciously sent and consciously received (see Ekman and Friesen 1969). If someone has just used an emblem and is asked to repeat it then they can reproduce the gesture quite easily. The vast majority of gestures are not, however, like emblems. They have no direct verbal translation. They do not substitute for words, rather they are produced alongside words. There is another major difference as well in that they are produced quite uncon-sciously as individuals speak. They are almost impossible to inhibit. Just watch someone gesturing with their free hand as they speak on the telephone, when the person that they are talking to clearly cannot see the hand movements being produced. I have a number of video-tapes of people speaking in a variety of types of conversation, where their hands are clearly out of sight of their interlocutors – for example, below the level of a table but nevertheless visible to the video-camera – and yet their hands still display an intricate and complex pattern. If you interrupt speakers while they are talking and ask them to reproduce these types of gesture they find it much more difficult to do so and sometimes quite impossible, depending on the type of gesture concerned. Now many psychologists consider these gestures to be a form of body language whose function is primarily to do with the expression of emotion or the signalling of interpersonal attitudes in social interaction. Occasionally, hand gestures do indeed have these functions. As I was driving to work today I saw a motorist in a silver BMW cut up another motorist on a notorious stretch of road where two lanes suddenly become one as you drive into Manchester. The second driver stopped abruptly and I noticed that his right hand formed a fist and made one staccato movement in the direction of the BMW driver. It seems that on occasion people don't so much shake their fist in anger, which is how we colloquially describe it, as thrust the fist forward. This was a hand movement that no doubt reflected intense emotion. Later when I was in work I noticed two colleagues displaying the same hand movement as each other. It was not just that the timing of their hand movements was perfectly synchronized, what we call interactional synchrony, but the precise form of the gesture and posture was also copied in a form of postural mirroring. My interpretation is that these behaviours reflect something about the relationship between the two people, although I would not dare to point this out to them. Sometimes hand gestures do seem to be part of body language and perform the functions traditionally assumed to be associated with it – the expression of emotions and the sometimes unconscious signalling of interpersonal relationships. But these were two isolated examples from a very long day. In between I witnessed literally thousands of other gestures about which many psychologists and all popular body language books have nothing substantial to say.

A female student was late with a course essay. She was discussing why she was unable to work in her student house. It was too noisy, too cold, too draughty, etc., etc. Her housemates were all English students, a little Byronic in their attitude. They sat around all night talking. She could not get to sleep. She sat in front of me with her hands tightly folded. Then as she started to talk her hands unfurled and started moving. She talked for about 15 minutes and my guess is that her hands were in perpetual motion for about 12 of those minutes. Unfortunately, I couldn't time the behaviour exactly. Nowhere in those 12 minutes did I detect a shaking fist or any interactional synchrony, just the hands moving alongside the speech, doing something – but what exactly?

Then my secretary came in to tell me about some important meetings that I must not miss ('The Dean wants to see you . . . The VC's secretary rang, he wants to know . . .') and this time I watched my secretary's hands moving in perfect synchrony with her speech, but again there did not appear to be much about emotion in these hand movements, nor much signalling of relationships. So it went on all through that day – hand movement after hand movement, gesture after gesture, all unconscious, all doing something. But it was not nonverbal communication, at least not in the traditional functional sense, as far as I could tell and, perhaps just as important, the movements did not appear to be separate from speech (remember Argyle and Trower's claim that 'humans use two quite separate languages, each with its own function'). The gestures seemed to be somehow connected with the speech itself. Where did that leave all the popular books on the subject?

I went home that night; I really did need a break, but there was no escape. I switched on *Better Homes* with Carol Vorderman. She started by introducing the programme and I reached for the button on my video-recorder. This is what she said. Note that I have split the complex behaviour into separate movements so that you can see how the movement closely integrates with the speech itself. The boundaries of each movement are marked by the [ ] brackets. You might like to try the movements yourself and consider why they might be relevant to what Carol Vorderman is saying.

'Welcome to *Better Homes*. This week we're in Leicester to give [a huge helping hand] [to some newly weds] [and a new mum].'

<u>Movement 1.</u> Hands are spread far apart with the palms facing downwards, the fingers are spread.
<u>Movement 2.</u> The thumb of the right hand points upwards, the fingers are clenched.
<u>Movement 3.</u> The index finger on the right hand is extended outwards, the thumb is pointing up. The other fingers are clenched.

She then met the builder that she was to be working with, and even in this short command the hands moved:

<u>'Carry on [young man].'</u>

<u>Movement 1.</u> Right arm is lifted to about head height and the palm of the right hand faces up, as if throwing something over the right shoulder.

Next she met the designer and again the hands were spontaneously called into action:

<u>'Dave said [I just want a shower] [that's all].'</u>

<u>Movement 1.</u> The right hand is at chest height, the fingers are together and the palm faces the designer. The right hand moves up and down, the left hand rests on her hip.
<u>Movement 2.</u> The palm of the right hand faces downwards with the fingers together. There is a sharp, sweeping movement of the hand from left to right.

I had had enough. I put on a nature programme, but there in front of me stood David Attenborough talking straight to the camera. I had to video-record it.

<u>'[This is the acorn of a white oak] [and this a red oak][only this] one is just slightly darker [but the acorns] [of the white oak germinate almost immediately] [using up] their food supply. [The red oaks] on the other hand [don't germinate until next spring]. [The squirrels recognise the difference between the two] and treat them differently.'</u>

There were nine distinguishable movements in this short extract, the boundaries of each marked by the square brackets. Just note how little of the speech was *not* accompanied by hand movement: 16 out of 58 words. That is, only 27.6 per cent of the words were *not* accompanied by hand movement.

Movement 1. The right hand is raised to just below shoulder level. The acorn is gripped between the index finger and the thumb; the other fingers are clenched.
Movement 2. The left hand is raised to mirror the right hand.
Movement 3. The hands are moved closer together until the acorns are almost touching. The little finger on the right hand is extended to point to the acorn in the left hand.
Movement 4. The left hand is lowered, the index finger and thumb of the right hand rotate the acorn so that it is closer to the face.
Movement 5. The right hand then moves up and down.
Movement 6. The left hand is raised up and the three remaining fingers are extended towards the acorn in the right hand.
Movement 7. Both hands are moved together just below shoulder height. The little finger of the right hand points to the acorn in the left hand. The remaining fingers of the left hand extend upwards.
Movement 8. Both hands are lowered slightly and spread apart, the fingers are together. The hands move up and down simultaneously.
Movement 9. The left hand is lowered out of shot and the right hand makes sharp up and down movements.

I went to make a cup of tea and came back to find David Attenborough crouching now and talking to the camera, but still moving his hands.

'And once [that has] gone the acorn will never germinate.'

<u>Movement 1.</u> The elbow of the left arm rests on the knee, the left hand then extends upwards with the fingers spread apart and pointing upwards.

Next he was sitting in a boat.

<u>'[A pool of] [deep] cold water like this.'</u>

<u>Movement 1.</u> The left arm extends out at just above waist height over the water. The palm of the left hand faces down with the fingers spread apart.
<u>Movement 2.</u> The left arm moves back slightly and the first gesture is repeated.

These movements of the hands and arms are gestures and you can see that these individual movements are closely integrated with the content of the speech itself. They are nearly always unconscious movements, even for experienced television presenters like David Attenborough. I will argue later in the book that we can potentially discriminate between unconscious movements produced naturally by the brain and those that are used consciously and deliberately by television presenters or people 'acting' in everyday life.

But the main point is clear – hand movement is a ubiquitous feature of everyday life. Those psychologists and body language popularizers who tell us that such movements are separate from language and perform essentially social functions are really missing the point. Some (and I mean a very small number) hand movements might reflect emotional state. The vast majority do no such thing and if you read almost any book with body language in the title you would be at a complete loss as to what they actually do. This book will hopefully explain exactly what they do and why they are uniquely important in reading another person.

'A remarkable biological miracle' 4

The subtitle of this book is *The New Psychology of Body Language* and yet in a sense some of the ideas about the importance of gesture in communication and as a medium for representing thought are far from new (see Kendon, 1982, for an excellent review of some of the historical issues). The first writings about gesture and speech and their connection are to be found in antiquity in Greek and Roman times. For Demosthenes, the Athenian statesman, military leader and orator, the delivery of a speech was at the very heart of oratory. Such delivery involved the whole body, but in particular it involved the hands working alongside the speech. According to the Roman statesman and philosopher Cicero, the 'action of the body' expresses 'the sentiments and passions of the soul'. In fact, the Latin word *actio* was Cicero's term for delivery. Cicero stated that 'nature has assigned to every emotion a particular look and tone of voice and bearing of its own; and the whole of a person's frame and every look on his face and utterance of his voice are like the strings of a harp, and sound according as they are struck by each successive emotion'. The body, according to Cicero, is like a musical instrument with the delivery or action being 'a sort of eloquence of the body, since it consists in gesticulation as well as speech' (see Kennedy, 1972).

The Greeks and Romans attempted to master this eloquence by studying and then prescribing the actions or movements to be made during the delivery of a speech. These prescribed actions or movements were quite exaggerated and would probably look quite alien to us today. This focus on gesture (and exaggeration of the form in terms of oratory) may have derived from the fact that, according to some scholars, the ancient Greeks and Romans relied more on gestures in everyday life and were somewhat better at reading them than we are today. For example, Wundt writes:

> The ancients were more familiar with the pleasure of gestures in casual communication than we are today. In fact, conventions actually demanded a superfluity of affective expression, whereas now we tend to suppress it. So the ancients had a more lively feel for the meaning of gestures, not because theirs was a more primitive culture, but simply because it differed from ours, and especially because the ability to discern outer signs of inner feeling was more developed.
>
> (Wundt 1921/1973: 66)

Condillac offers a wonderful commentary on the work of the ancient Greeks and Romans on gesture and rhetoric and how it might be viewed from a contemporary perspective (at least from the contemporary perspective of 18th-century France):

> We do not value an actor except so far as he commands the art of expressing all the emotions of the soul by a slight variation of gestures, and find him unnatural if he deviates too much from our usual gesticulation. For that reason we can no longer have fixed principles to regulate all the attitudes and movements that are used in declamation.
>
> (Condillac 1756/2001: 133)

For Cicero, the attitudes and movements of actors could be regulated for maximum effect but, according to Condillac, in Greek and Roman times they went even further than this 'by dividing the chant and the gestures between two actors. This practice may seem extraordinary, but we see how one actor, by a measured movement, could appropriately vary his attitudes to make them agree with the narrative of the other who did the declamation, and why they would be as shocked by a gesture out of measure as we are by the steps of a dancer who does not keep time' (1756/2001: 133). Condillac also points out that it was only in scenes of dialogue that a comic actor would continue to do both gesture and narration, otherwise the narration and gesture would be split between two actors. The reason for this, according to Condillac, is that 'his action gained in liveliness because his energies were not divided'. In other words in antiquity the natural association between speech and gesture was split. The practice of dividing communication in this way led to the discovery of the art of mime and to the continued exaggeration and prescription of the movements to be used in communication with gesture.

Quintilian in the first century AD discusses gesture in his work *Institutiones Oratoriae*. One section of his work involved specifying the kinds of gestures to be used by orators as they gave their speeches; detailed instructions were provided as to how the gestures should be used by orators to achieve the maximum effect (see Kendon, 1982, p. 46). Quintilian stresses the similarities, including similarities in function, between gestures and speech when he states: 'For other portions of the body merely help the speaker, whereas the hands may almost be said to speak. Do we not use them to demand, promise, summon, dismiss, threaten, supplicate, express aversion or fear, question or deny?' (100/1902: 85–6).

The kinds of gestures being discussed here, while still being hand movements used to accompany talk, are really quite different from those we shall consider in this book in that they are, like language itself, to be carefully, intentionally and consciously produced. We are concerned with the *spontaneous* gestures produced without careful consideration and therefore much more revealing of a speaker's thoughts.

It was in the seventeenth century that the first academic works exclusively on the use of gesture started to appear. The earliest work in English was a book by Bulwer (1644/

1974) entitled *Chirologia-Chironomia*. The first part is a descriptive glossary of 64 gestures of the hand and 25 gestures of the fingers. Bulwer not only describes each gesture in considerable detail but also the affective, cognitive or physiological state associated with that gesture. He outlines one or two variants of the gesture and then offers an interpretation of each one. The second part of the book is a prescriptive guide that outlines the proper usage of an additional 81 gestures during well-delivered discourse. He cautions against the improper use of 'manual rhetoricke' (see Morrel-Samuels 1990 for a review of Bulwer).

The next major work on gesture, written in English, is Austin's *Chironomia* (1806/1966). This book includes a detailed consideration of gestures and their effects on an audience, with examples to practice appropriate delivery. This book had a significant influence on the textbooks written over the next century designed for instruction in the art of elocution in schools.

In addition to such practical interest in gesture there was also a bourgeoning philosophical interest, which recognized the importance of gesture in our understanding of human beings and the human mind, and this is evident in, amongst other works, Bacon's *Advancement of Learning* (1605/1952). Bacon argues that gestures provide an indication of the state of the mind of the speaker and of the will: 'As the tongue speaketh to the ear, so the gesture speaketh to the eye' (1605/1952: 49). In fact Bulwer explicitly acknowledges that is is Bacon's exact words here that inspired him to produce his own great work on gesture. A major reason why Bulwer found gesture of such interest was because he thought of it as a 'natural' language in sharp contrast to the artificiality and arbitrariness of ordinary verbal language. He states that 'gesture is the only speech and general language of the human nature . . . It speaks all languages, and as a universal character of reason, is generally understood and known by all nations' (1644/1974: 3).

The idea that gesture should be studied because it is a natural form of human action and expression which may throw light on the origin of language, and ultimately on the content of the human soul, was introduced by Etienne Bonnot De Condillac (1756/2001). His classic text argues against the 17th-century Cartesian view that human reason and knowledge are innate, given by God himself. As Aarslef (2001) states: 'In the Cartesian view, innateness owes no debt to social intercourse. Right reason and knowledge are private achievements, for in the Augustinian sense we do not truly learn anything from anybody. God alone is the teacher. Communication is risky' (2001: xii). Condillac, on the other hand – while still believing that 'Adam and Eve did not owe the exercise of the operations of their soul to experience. As they came from the hands of God, they were able, by special assistance, to reflect and communicate their thoughts to each other. But I am assuming that two children, one of either sex, sometime after the deluge, had gotten lost in the desert before they would have known the use of any sign' (1756/2001: 113) – held that communication derives from action and experience and that the mimes found in performance in the time of the Emperor Augustus had brought their art to such perfection that they could perform whole plays by gesture alone, thus unawares creating 'a language which had been the first that mankind spoke'. Human language, after the deluge, came about as an exchange of natural gestures to which vocalizations later became associated and Condillac attempted to describe how this process might have proceeded.

Diderot believed that the original nature of language might be understood through the study of the expressions of deaf-mutes. Indeed, he states that 'a man born deaf and dumb has no prejudices with regard to the manner of communicating his thoughts. Consider that inversions have not passed into his language from another, and that if he uses them it is nature alone which suggests their use' (1751/ 1916: 166–7). This philosophical position meant that the sign language of the deaf would be of considerable interest. In 1774 Abbé L'Epée began his important work with the use of sign language in the education of the deaf. He taught them French by focusing on the use of manual signs, rather than by attempting to force them to produce any vocal output.

However, this was not the approach used elsewhere. For example, in England at this time people who could not speak were not that sympathetically treated, and were seen as not fully functioning in God's image. Methods of instruction for deaf people in England focused on the vocal–auditory channels rather than the manual channel.

In the 19th century interest grew in both scientific and philosophical aspects of gesture and what gestures may reveal (see Kendon 1982 for a review). Tylor (1878), one of the founders of contemporary anthropology, explicitly focused on 'gesture language' and considered what variations in gestures across cultures might tell us about the characteristics of the human mind. His conclusion was that gesture language 'tends to prove that the mind of the uncultured man works in much the same way at all times everywhere' (1878: 88).

Wundt, regarded by many as the 'father of experimental psychology', was another leading scientific figure to consider gesture. Indeed his volume *The Language of Gestures* is a classic in the field. In this monograph he anticipates many of the core theoretical questions that we will consider in this book. He is explicitly concerned with the relationship between gestures and thinking:

> It is customary to define gestural communication as an 'expression of thought through visible but not audible movements' and, accordingly, to allot this gestural means of expression a place between script and speech. Like the former, it depicts concepts by means of visible signs, although signs pass quickly, as speech sounds do. Thus gestures appear as pictorial script, or letters, with which its symbols are sketched in the air by means of transitory signs, rather than on a solid material which could preserve them.
>
> (Wundt 1921/1973: 55)

Wundt was solely concerned with gestures that become conventionalised among various people or communities, including Indian tribes, Cistercian monks, Neapolitan society or deaf mutes. He examines how particular gestures come to represent specific properties of the world and how some gestures, through 'intervening associative links', come to represent more abstract categories; for example:

> Moving the finger from the eye of the person communicating toward that of another person or from heart to heart signifies agreement of disposition or view among the Indians; and there is the sign for 'anger', as used by the Cistercians: moving both hands quickly away from the heart to stimulate the welling up and overflowing of feeling.
>
> (Wundt 1921/1973: 91)

One interesting point is that Wundt held that 'the primary cause of natural gestures does not lie in the motivation to communicate a concept, but rather in the expression of an emotion' (1921/1973: 146), a view that you could say has held sway for more than a century in terms of general work in nonverbal communication. Wundt is fascinating on gesture and, as I have already stated, he anticipates many of the issues raised by more contemporary writers, but what he ignores (except in the most general terms) are the rich, spontaneous gestures that people generate in their everyday lives, as they create meaning with their hands. He was interested in the gestures that all members of a community would recognize and be able to interpret correctly and in the syntax, in terms of word order, which would allow them to do this efficiently and effectively. His conclusions certainly do have a contemporary ring about them: 'Language, and before that, gestural communication, is a faithful mirror of man in the totality of his psychic achievements' (1921/1973: 148–9). In this book, we will consider some of the psychic achievements of mankind in their *spontaneous* use of speech and gesture *simultaneously*.

Other scholars have commented on the fact that the movement of the hands, whether in the form of gesture or not, can be highly revealing in everyday life. Such scholars include both Sigmund Freud and the anthropologist and linguist Edward Sapir. Freud famously suggests: 'He that has eyes to see and ears to hear may convince himself that no mortal can keep a secret. If his lips are silent, he chatters with his fingertips' (1905/1953: 77–8). Sapir argues for the existence of a collective 'unconscious', that is a set of rules or a grammar which everyone applies in bodily expression without being able to make the rules explicit: 'We respond to gestures with an extreme alertness and, one might almost say, in accordance with an elaborate and secret code that is written nowhere, known by none, and understood by all' (1927/1949: 556).

The study of gesture is by no means new, but the majority of systematic work on the subject has been either from the perspective of oratory, in which gesture is to be regarded as a resource to be used deliberately and intentionally in the delivery of a speech, or from the perspective of the language of the deaf where gesture is to be regarded as the only resource that can be used in communication. Many influential figures have commented on gestures but have not necessarily studied them in their natural, spontaneous state – i.e. in terms of their close natural connections with the underlying verbal channel – in sufficient detail really to understand them; except perhaps in the case of Wundt, although he restricted himself to gestures that have become conventionalized. The early observations of Cicero and Quintilian to some extent led to the gestural system becoming disembodied from its natural speech context (and only extraordinarily being reintegrated in time by different speakers in a performance). Rather surprisingly, over the past two millennia the gesture–speech connection has been largely neglected in the case of *spontaneous* gesture, despite the huge growth of recent interest in spontaneous nonverbal communication.

Writing in 1982 Adam Kendon presents an interesting argument for the relative neglect of the study of gesture generally, and spontaneous gesture in particular, despite the enormous interest in nonverbal communication. His argument quite simply is that gesture was never considered a very good example of 'nonverbal communication' and therefore it was left to one side. 'Nonverbal communication' was a concept that relied heavily on the work of Jurgen Ruesch in a number of important papers published in the 1950s (1953, 1955), in which he applied information theory and cybernetics to the analysis of human social interaction. As Kendon says:

> Once human action was conceived of as if it were a code in an information transmission system, the question of the nature of the coding system came under scrutiny. Much was made of the distinction between analogical codes and digital codes. Aspects of behavior such as facial expression and bodily movement, which appeared to vary in a continuous fashion, was said to encode information analogically. This included gesture, insofar as it was thought of as 'pictoral' and the indexical character of much gesturing was also clearly of an analogical nature. The sharp dichotomy that this distinction between the two kinds of encoding in human behavior proposed gave rise to the concept of 'nonverbal communication'. Such communication was seen as employing devices quite different from those of spoken language and it was regarded as having sharply different functions. 'Nonverbal communication' was seen as having to do with the processes by which interpersonal relations are established and maintained, whereas the digital codes of spoken language were concerned with conveying propositional information.
>
> (Kendon 1982: 53)

As I have already pointed out, the anthropologist Gregory Bateson developed this notion. But what about gesture? Well, Ruesch himself was not particularly clear as to what to do with gesture, sometimes considering it to be like language and at other times including it with other forms of 'nonverbal codification'. According to Kendon:

In the expansion of research that followed, attention was directed in the main, to aspects of behaviour that clearly did not have the functions of spoken language. Gesture, though often referred to, was little investigated in the tradition because, as Ruesch himself seemed to be aware, it was less clearly involved in the functions that had been postulated for 'nonverbal communication' and it seemed to have a close association with verbal expression.

(Kendon 1982: 54)

In the years following the work of Ruesch and Bateson there was a huge explosion in research in linguistics and psychology on both written and spoken language and in psychology on nonverbal communication, but gesture, as Kendon puts it, 'fell between two stools'. There it lay relatively neglected and under-researched but invariably categorized as part of nonverbal communication – body language – with implications about its possible function. It remained quite neglected until a number of things happened.

First, a linguist called Noam Chomsky (1957) developed new ideas about the nature of human language, arguing that human language has certain identifiable characteristics which make it essentially and uniquely human and qualitatively different from communication in any other species. Chomsky stressed the creativity of language (Hockett's design feature of 'productivity'). The majority of utterances we produce are ones we have never spoken in precisely that form before and the majority of utterances we hear and comprehend without difficulty are ones we have never heard before.

'*Big Brother* psychologist falls off his chair in his dingy, dusty attic as he reached for the red pencil on the left of his desk as he wrote this book' is a wonderfully creative (and accurate) utterance; wonderfully creative at least in the technical sense we are discussing here, probably generated for the first time in the history of mankind. I generated it effortlessly and you probably understood it without any trouble. You can see me now lying on that floor, trying to pick myself up, covered in dust. Chomsky put great emphasis on the creativity of language and argued that such creativity can only be explained if we credit speakers not with a repertoire of learned responses, which was how behavioural psychologists up to that point were attempting to explain it, but with a repertoire of linguistic rules used to generate or interpret sentences. Chomsky also argued that any theory of language must also explain why some speakers feel some sentences to be 'related' and others 'unrelated'. The following four sentences are all rather different in form, yet speakers accept them as closely related:

1. 'The psychologist who works for *Big Brother* started work on a new book.'
2. 'Did the psychologist who works for *Big Brother* start work on a new book?'
3. 'A new book was started by the psychologist who works for *Big Brother.*'
4. 'Was a new book started by the psychologist who works for *Big Brother*?'

In contrast, two sentences may be identical in form yet feel very different, for example:

5. 'My son is difficult to wash.'
6. 'My son is reluctant to wash.'

In (5) my son is on the receiving end of the wash whereas in (6) he is the one doing the wash. Similarly, to use one of Chomsky's oft-quoted examples, 'William is easy to please' and 'William is eager to please' have similar surface structures but do not feel closely related because in the former William is the one being pleased whereas in the latter he is the one doing the pleasing. Chomsky's solution to this dilemma is to propose that every sentence can be described at two levels – at a surface structure level, i.e. how it actually is produced, and at a deep or underlying structure level. Sentences (1) to (4) concerning the *Big Brother* psychologist and the book have different surface structures but the same deep structure. According to Chomsky, that is why these sentences are felt to be closely related. In contrast, sentences (5) and (6) about my son's attitude to washing have the same surface structure but different deep structures and are therefore felt to be distantly related (like the two sentences about pleasing William).

Take an ambiguous sentence like 'Striking miners can be dangerous.' This sentence can be interpreted in at least three different ways (and in three additional ways in spoken English if we include the homophone 'minor' as well), namely:

1. Miners who are on strike can be dangerous.
2. It can be dangerous to strike miners.
3. Miners who are striking (in appearance) can be dangerous.

For Chomsky, ambiguous sentences are ambiguous because they permit two or more different deep structures from the same surface structure, one deep structure related to each interpretation. The deep structure is a description of the sentence's underlying grammatical or syntactical structure (in the above example 'striking' can be either an adjective or a verb and is therefore connected in different ways to the underlying grammatical structure of the sentence). This deep structure clearly affects its meaning (for further discussion see Ellis and Beattie 1986).

Chomsky also claims that we can move between related sentences to form different types of sentence. Such moves are called transformations; for example, we can move from sentence (1) to (2), on page 55, to form a question using a specific type of operation, but the important point here is that this operation recognizes the underlying grammatical structure of the sentence. Chomsky calls these types of operation 'structure-dependent' operations, where each structure-dependent operation 'considers not merely the sequence of elements that constitute the sentence, but also their structure' (1972: 29); in this case that the sequence 'the psychologist who works for *Big Brother*' is a particular type of phrase called a noun phrase. Chomsky argues that all human languages use such structure-dependent operations. Although children make certain kinds of error in the course of language learning, they do not make the mistake of applying rules other than the structure-dependent one. His conclusion is that structure-dependent rules 'are a priori for the species' and therefore innate. Such rules, he argues, do not derive from experience. This theory, of course, is a form of neo-Cartesianism and contrasts markedly with the views of anti-Cartesians like Condillac, whom we met earlier, and the views of the empiricists of today. According to Chomsky, we may all speak with different tongues but we have one uniquely human mind, and that mind is to be understood through the analysis and description of these linguistic rules if we are to understand what knowledge is innate.

The theoretical work of Noam Chomsky transformed psychology. It led to the rejection of behaviourism as a serious framework for the study of complex mental functions like language and heralded a new era in the search for the rules and principles that underpin all human cognitive activity. It led to the birth of cognitive psychology, to use one metaphor, or the cognitive revolution, to use another. Somewhat paradoxically, it also led other researchers to attempt to determine if other species could develop language with the same unique properties as human language. Were we human beings really quite alone, as Chomsky thought? Could, for example, chimpanzees learn some form of human language and display creativity in the use of that language, just like human beings? We already knew that chimpanzees in the wild are capable of displaying a wide range of communicative signals, including a range of calls and facial expressions (Marler and Tenaza 1977; van Lawick-Goodall 1971), with each signal communicating something of the internal state of the animal. A soft barking noise indicates annoyance or mild aggressiveness towards another, while a 'grin' with the mouth closed or only slightly open indicates submission or fright. But these were limited forms of communication. Given the right circumstances, could chimpanzees use language creatively? Could they learn rules to combine words into new sentences just like human beings? The answer was yes and no (see Gardner and Gardner 1978). They did display some degree of creativity, but not quite like human beings, and the theoretical import of the work has been hotly contested (see Chomsky 1976).

Washoe was a young chimp reared by Allen and Beatrice Gardner in as 'childlike' a manner as possible, where her caretakers used a sign language based on the American Sign Language of the US deaf community. In Washoe's case the acquisition of the basic language took about four years. Her 'words', like the words of sign language, were gestural signs; for example, holding the fingertips of one hand together and touching the nose with them meant 'flower', while repeatedly touching the fingertips together meant 'more'. By the age of around six years Washoe was credited with some 160 signs, which she would combine into communicative utterances such as 'gimme flower', 'more fruit', 'tickle Washoe', 'comb black' or 'baby mine'. The Gardners also noted that Washoe learned signs that involved touching parts of her own body quicker than signs which were merely traced in the air, possibly because of the tactile reinforcement from the skin touched. Washoe's achievements were considerable. Kortlandt writing in 1973 comments:

> The Gardners generously allowed me to watch Washoe in some experimental sessions at an age when, according to them, she had already 'spoken' more than 100 different gestural words. I was deeply impressed by what I saw. Perhaps the most convincing of all was to watch Washoe 'reading' an illustrated magazine. When, for example, a vermouth advertisement appeared, she spontaneously made the gesture for 'drink'; when, on the next page, a picture of a tiger appeared, she signed

'cat'. It was fascinating to see a chimpanzee 'thinking aloud' in gestural language, but in perfect silence, and without being rewarded for her performance in such a situation.

(Kortlandt 1973/1992: 74)

Gardner and Gardner (1978) themselves did not under-estimate what they had managed to achieve through their intensive coaching of a young chimpanzee; nor were they inclined to underestimate the theoretical significance of what had occurred:

> The results of Project Washoe present the first serious challenge to the traditional doctrine that only human beings could have language . . . [Washoe] learned a natural human language and her early utterances were highly similar to, perhaps indistinguishable from, the early utter-ances of human children. Now, the categorical question, can a nonhuman being use a human language must be replaced with quantitative ques-tions; how much language, how soon, or how far can they go.
>
> (Gardner and Gardner 1978: 73)

The claims of the Gardners and other ape language researchers have not, however, gone unchallenged (e.g. Seidenberg and Petito 1979; Terrace 1979). As Andrew Ellis and I have written in the past, no one seriously doubts that chimps can associate together meanings and arbitrary signs both in comprehension and in production, but most people would want to say that there is more to language than naming. Language orders its words into structures – rule-governed sentences. Sentence structure indicates how named concepts relate one to another. English uses word order for this purpose, so that '*Big Brother* psychologist teases the chimp' means something different from 'The chimp teases the *Big Brother* psychologist'. There is no strong evidence for consistent, productive use of word order or any similar grammatical device by any of the signing chimps. Terrace's (1979) chimp Nim Chimpsky (a name rather like Noam Chomsky don't you think?) had a preference for putting certain signs in certain positions (e.g. 'more' at the beginning of sign sequences, and his own name at the end), but otherwise his choice of sign order was quite random.

A feature of animal displays in the wild is their extreme repetitiveness. Wilson writes:

> If a zoologist were required to select just one word that characterizes animal communication systems, he might well settle on 'redundancy'. Animal displays as they really occur in nature tend to be very repetitious, in extreme cases approaching the point of what seems like inanity to the human observer.
>
> (Wilson 1975: 200)

Such repetition (e.g. 'Me banana you banana me give you') was characteristic of Washoe and other signing apes, though it is largely absent from the language of young deaf or hearing children. Ape signing is also highly imitative. Close analysis of Nim's signing at the age of two years revealed that 38 per cent of his signs were imitations of signs recently used by his caretakers. Unlike the imitations of children, which are far fewer than this and decline with age, Nim's imitative signs reached 54 per cent in words by the age of four years. Further, only 12 per cent of Nim's utterances initiated interactions; the remainder were produced in response to prodding by his teachers.

Other criticisms levelled at the chimp research include an excessive reliance on a small number of oft-repeated anecdotes; somewhat generous criteria for what constituted a correct response in formalized naming experiments, the possible contribution of natural, unlearned gestures and the lack of extensive, 'raw' transcripts of chimpanzee conversation. Perhaps the most intriguing criticism is the paradox by Chomsky himself when he writes:

In some ill-considered popularizations of interesting current research, it is virtually argued that higher apes have the capacity for language but have never put it to use – a remarkable biological miracle, given the enormous selectional advantage of even minimal linguistic skills, rather like discovering that some animal has wings but has never thought to fly.

(Chomsky 1976: 40)

If chimps are capable of acquiring language, why have they not done so of their own accord? The only viable counter to this argument is to propose that the natural lifestyle of chimps is one that does not require language. Hewes (1973a, 1973b) and Kortlandt (1973/1992) have suggested that only with the switch from fruit picking to hunting did language become advantageous to man because of the group co-ordination needed. Put quite simply, Kortlandt claims that fruit pickers 'have less to discuss with one another than co-operative big game hunters'. But this is just one view as to how verbal language developed in man. Darwin in *The Expression of the Emotions in Man and Animals* suggests that verbal language has developed using 'sound-producing organs . . . first developed for sexual purposes, in order that one sex might call or charm the other' (1872: 355).

So we can see that this work with chimpanzees had one other direct effect. It led to serious speculation about the origins of language for the first time in perhaps a century. (In 1866 the Societé de Linguistique de Paris had banned papers speculating about the origins of language. These papers were very much prompted by Darwin's convincing case made in *The Origin of Species* (1859) for the evolution of man from more primitive species.) But now it was no longer the case that, as Charles Hockett (1978) put it, 'one person's whimsy was as good as another's'.

In a seminal paper Gordon Hewes (1973a/1992) presents a coherent argument that the first form of language must have been gestural in form and the chimpanzee research by the Gardners is critical to his argument. He suggests that some early precursors of man, the australopithicenes, had similar brain size and cultural accomplishment to existing chimpanzees and gorillas and therefore 'it is reasonable to credit the australopithecines with at least the cognitive capacities of existing chimpanzees or gorillas' (1992: 66). Existing chimpanzees could acquire a creative gestural language (with considerable effort it should be said); therefore early man probably had the capacity for a gestural language. Speech, on the other hand, would have required a good deal of brain reorganization before it could become dominant. Therefore Hewes argued that 'a preexisting gestural language system would have provided an easier pathway to vocal language than a direct outgrowth of the "emotional" use of vocalization characteristic of non-human primates' (1992: 72). His argument is that speech as a system of communication (Hockett's design feature of 'use of the vocal–auditory channel') had a number of significant evolutionary advantages over manual gesture and that is why it became predominant:

> the vocal–auditory channel is practically a clear channel for communication, whereas the visual channel, as the prime modality for human and all higher primate perception of the external world, is subject to continual interference from nonlanguage sources. Unambiguous decoding of gestural messages requires a fairly neutral background, good illumination, absence of intervening objects (including foliage), relatively short distance between transmitter and receiver, and frontal orientation. Making manual gestures is slower than speaking, requires more energy, and prevents the use of the hands for any other activity while the message is being transmitted; decoding sign-language message is also slower, even among trained deaf persons.
> (Hewes 1992: 70)

Hewes also presents a further interesting argument, that gesture:

did not merely persist as a kind of older, retarded brother of speech, but gained a new lease of life in the Upper Paleolithic period and thereafter, with the birth of drawing, painting and sculpture, as Leroi-Gourhan (1964–5) and others have observed. Such art forms can be regarded as 'frozen gestures', akin to the air-pictures of sign language, but traced or formed in durable media.

(Hewes 1992: 71)

This old visual–gestural channel, Hewes argues, became 'the preferred mode for advanced propositional communication in higher mathematics, physics, chemistry, biology and other sciences and technology, in the familiar forms of algebraic signs, molecular structure diagrams, flow-charts, maps, symbolic logic, wiring or circuit diagrams, and all the other ways we represent complex variables, far beyond the capacity of the linear bursts of speech sounds' (Hewes 1992: 71).

According to Hewes, this is where gesture ended up – as a system to be used in more complex and more specialized communication but not in everyday communication where speech was triumphant: 'The vocal–auditory channel continues to serve the needs of close, interpersonal, face-to-face communication, in song, poetry, drama, religious ritual, or persuasive political discourse.' He draws attention to the somewhat sparse literature on how gesture and speech relate in everyday talk and argues:

Gesture did not wither away, but persisted as a common accompaniment of speech, either as a kinesic paralanguage for conveying nuances, emphasis or even contradiction of the spoken message (Birdwhistell, 1970, La Barre, 1964, Hall, 1959) or in situations where spoken language fails because of inaudibility in noisy places or, more often, where there is no common tongue.

(Hewes 1992: 71)

But just look at the terms he uses when he describes the use of gesture in everyday talk – 'not wither away', 'common accompaniment of speech', 'where spoken language fails'; gesture here is very much second best.

Thus because of developments elsewhere, the system that had not 'withered away' became interesting and important, all because of a young American linguist called Noam Chomsky (he was only 29 years old when his first major book, *Syntactic Structures*, was published in 1957) and those determined to prove him wrong with a couple of chimpanzees and several years of intensive tuition. This new research into hand gestures revealed a great deal more than could have been imagined at that time. It was not just about nuance or about communication in noisy places, but an essential and integral part of all communication; indeed some might say as much a biological miracle as language itself.

Images in the hands, images in the mind 5

There are a number of different types of gesture that are produced quite unconsciously and appear commonly with everyday speech.

Iconic gestures

The first type are called *iconic* gestures. These are gestures whose particular form displays a close relationship to the meaning of the accompanying speech. For example, when describing a scene from a comic book story in which a character bends a tree back to the ground, the speaker appears to grip something and pull it back. This is called an iconic gesture because it refers to the same act mentioned in the speech; the gesture seems to be connected to the words 'and he bends it way back'. This particular example comes from David McNeill's seminal book *Hand and Mind* (1992: 12). I should point out before showing this example that (following the conventions introduced by McNeill) through-out this book the speech actually said is underlined in the text. The boundaries of the meaningful part of the gesture (the so-called 'stroke' phase of the gesture), unless other-wise stated, are shown by enclosing the concurrent seg-ments of speech in square brackets, like this [ ]. The gesture accompanying the clause 'and he bends it way back' was as follows; the brackets indicate where the important bit of the gesture occurred:

and he [bends it way back]
Iconic: hand appears to grip something and pull it from the upper front space back and down near to the shoulder.

This example illustrates the close connection that exists between speech and gesture, the close connection between language and this form of nonverbal communication, which are clearly not separate, as many psychologists have assumed. These iconic gestures only occur during the act of speaking itself, although they are sometimes initiated during the brief silent or planning pauses in the speech; they are not made by listeners except very occasionally. The example shows how what is depicted in the gesture should be incorporated into a complete picture of a person's thought process. The sentence describes the tree being bent 'way back'; the gesture at the same time depicts a bending-back image. The gesture clearly adds meaning here because it shows how the bending back is accomplished and it shows it from the point of view of the agent, the person doing the bending back. The gesture shows that the tree is fastened at one end, which is not made explicit in the accompanying speech.

As David McNeill himself says: 'Speech and gesture refer to the same event and are partially overlapping, but the pictures they present are different. Jointly, speech and gesture give a more complete insight.' Notice also that the gesture is produced at exactly the same time as the speech. It is not that the speaker says the words and then decides to illustrate it with a gesture; the two forms of communication are generated simultaneously by the human brain. Also notice that there is no problem in generating the speech; it is not the case that the speaker is trying to compensate for some defect in the linguistic communication.

What is interesting about this iconic gesture is that not only does it reveal the speaker's mental image about the event in question, but it also reveals the particular point of view that he has taken towards it. The speaker had the choice of depicting the event from the viewpoint of the agent or of the tree itself. In performing this particular gesture the speaker was clearly 'seeing' the event from the viewpoint of the agent because otherwise his hand would not have taken the form of a grip. If the speaker had been taking the viewpoint of the tree, the hand would have simply depicted the bend backwards without the grip.

Consider another example of an iconic gesture, also from McNeill (1992: 13):

And she [chases him out again]
Iconic: hand appears to swing an object through the air.

Again the speech and gesture refer to the same event and are partially overlapping but again the pictures they present are different. The speech conveys the idea of pursuit ('chases') and repetition ('again') but the speech does not mention what she is chasing him with. The iconic gesture conveys that some form of weapon is being used here because the iconic gesture depicts something being swung through the air. The iconic gesture does not tell us exactly what the object is at this point but we can see quite clearly what kind of object it is. The gesture shows that it is a long object, which can be gripped by a hand, and it is something that can be swung through the air. It is in fact an umbrella. The significant point is that if we were to focus exclusively on the speech, as we do on the telephone, for example, or only on the gesture, then we would have an incomplete picture of the speaker's mental representation of the scene. It is only through a consideration of both forms of communication that we see all of the elements depicted: the agent, the type of action, the repetition of the action, the type of weapon used and how the weapon was actually being used – swung through the air to frighten the other character.

Below is an example from my own corpus of speech and gestures, where I used a similar task to that of McNeill, asking participants to narrate cartoon stories to a listener, without mentioning that the focus of the research was gestures. The advantage of asking people to narrate stories such as cartoons is that we can compare their gesture–speech combinations with what was in the original story to see exactly what was included in their communication and what was left out. Cartoon stories have the additional advantage that depicted in them are a lot of interesting characters doing a wide variety of complex actions.

[she's eating the food]
Iconic: fingers on left hand are close together, palm is facing body, and thumb is directly behind index finger. Hand moves from waist level towards mouth.

The speech here tells us that the agent is female. It also conveys the nature of the action involved ('eating') and what is being eaten ('the food'), but it does not tell us how this action is being accomplished. There are after all many different ways of eating food. She could be just chewing the food, which is already in her mouth, or using a knife and fork to eat the food from a plate, but she is not. In this cartoon story she was drawing the food with her left hand up towards her mouth. That is how the action was depicted in the original cartoon and that is how the narrator depicts it in his gesture. The iconic gesture again is critical to communication here because it shows the method of eating – bringing the food to the mouth with the hand. Again, the image depicted was from the point of view of the agent; the hand of the speaker is acting as the hand of the character in the cartoon.

When you consider all of this, it is extraordinary that people have tried to dismiss the movements of the hands and arms which people make when they speak as merely coincidental movements – virtually random flicks and twirls that are merely used for emphasis, merely used to make a point and barely worthy of serious consideration. Alternatively they are thought of as a relatively minor form of nonverbal communication with a fairly insignificant role in the communication of emotion or interpersonal attitudes. Many psychologists argue that this is the main point of nonverbal communication, and quite inferior to the more obvious forms of nonverbal communication such as bodily posture, facial expression or eye gaze, which are clearly more important in this regard.

But these movements are not insignificant, and they are not merely poor forms of communication about emotion or interpersonal attitudes. They are closely integrated with speech and may provide a unique insight into how speakers are actually thinking.

Let us consider the issue of the integration of speech and gesture in a little more detail. A prototypical iconic gesture involves three phases: first, the preparation phase, where the hand rises from its resting place and moves to the front of the body and away from the speaker in preparation to make the gesture; second, there is the main part of the gesture, the so-called 'stroke' phase where the gesture exhibits its meaning; third, there is the retraction phase where the hand moves back to its rest position. Some gestures, however, have just two phases and some possess just a stroke phase. The example below, from McNeill (1992: 25), shows the preparation and the stroke phase of this gesture:

he grabs a big oak tree and he [bends it way back]
　　　　　　　　　(1)　　　　　　　　(2)
(1)　*Preparation phase: hand rises from armrest of chair and moves up and forward at eye level, assuming a grip shape at the same time.*
(2)　*Stroke phase: hand appears to pull something backwards and downwards, ending up near the shoulder.*

Gestures in their preparation phase anticipate that part of the speech which refers to the same event. Indeed, this observation led another pioneer in the gesture area, Brian Butterworth, now Professor of Neurospychology at the University of London, to suggest that we can actually distinguish iconic gestures that are used alongside speech for intentional effect rather than being used spontaneously by the fact that the preparation phase of intentional gestures does not anticipate the speech in this natural manner. An example he was fond of using was archive footage of Harold Macmillan, former UK Prime Minister, who sometimes made iconic gestures when he spoke in his early television broadcasts to suggest, presumably, informality and spontaneity, but these gestures did not display the necessary degree of anticipation of the verbal content. In some research I carried out with Brian Butterworth as a student at Cambridge, we found that the average amount of time that spontaneous gestures precede the noun or verb with which they are most closely associated is in the order of 800 milliseconds (see Beattie 1983). Harold Macmillan's gestures did not show this degree of anticipation, or indeed any degree of anticipation. Consequently, they looked false and almost certainly were false, owing more to Quintilian and work on classic rhetoric than the human mind in spontaneous action.

The anticipation of the verbal content by a spontaneous iconic gesture can be seen in the example below (see Beattie and Aboudan 1994 for related examples). Here the narrator is telling a cartoon story about the exploits of 'Headless Harry', who goes fishing in a river with a rod but has no luck, so the head decides to frighten the fish out of the water. But the head then falls into the water and has to swim along back to the body. This particular gesture has a preparation phase, a stroke phase and a retraction phase as follows:

<u>the head starts [swimming] along</u>
$\qquad$(1)$\qquad$(2)$\qquad$(3)

(1) *Preparation phase: index finger of right hand originally touching temple, hand moves forward with fingers opening, palm facing downwards at level of shoulder.*

(2) *Stroke phase: right hand indicates the way that the head is swimming in the water, focusing on forward motion with splayed fingers representing the head.*

(3) *Retraction phase: right hand moves back to temple, to exactly the same start point, index finger straightens up.*

The preparation phase of this iconic gesture in which the hand takes on the shape to represent a head swimming was 440 milliseconds in duration. The stroke phase during which the hand shows how the head was swimming along was 240 milliseconds long. The retraction phase during which the hand returns to the original start position was the longest phase at 600 milliseconds. In all, there was just over a second's worth of complex hand movement during which the mind unconsciously portrayed how the head of a ghost propelled itself in a river before returning the hand to exactly the same resting position that it had started from just over a second earlier.

The analysis of the phases of gesture and how they relate to speech demonstrate the close integration of these two channels of communication. They are not separate and they are also not separate in terms of their sequence of development in childhood or in terms of how they break down together with the brain damage that produce a type of speech disorder called aphasia. Iconic gestures develop alongside language when children are learning to talk, with iconic gestures developing at the same time as the early phrases in speech are used. As Susan Goldin-Meadow notes:

> At a time in their development when children are limited in what they can say, there is another avenue of expression open to them, one that can extend the range of ideas they are able to express. In addition to speaking, the child can also gesture (Bates 1976; Bates *et al.* 1979; Petitto 1988).
>
> (Goldin-Meadow 1999: 118)

Children usually begin gesturing at around ten months of age, using pointing gestures (called 'deictics') whose meaning is given by the context rather than by their precise form – the child may point to an object to draw the adult's attention to it. It is only later that children begin to use iconic gestures, which capture aspects of the form of the object or action and are thus less reliant on specific context to give meaning to the particular gesture. Goldin-Meadow argues that the integration of gesture and speech can be identified in the very earliest stages of linguistic development, that is, at the one-word stage:

Over time, children become proficient users of their spoken language. At the same time, rather than dropping out of children's communicative repertoires, gesture itself continues to develop and play an important role in communication. Older children frequently use hand gestures as they speak (Jancovic, Devoe and Wiener 1975), gesturing, for example, when asked to narrate a story (McNeill 1992) or when asked to explain their reasoning on a series of problems (Church and Goldin-Meadow 1986).

(Goldin-Meadow 1999: 120–1)

This integration continues until adulthood. When communication starts to break down with the brain damage that produces different types of aphasia, the two channels break down in strikingly similar ways. For example, in Wernicke's aphasia, patients produce fluent speech that has little appropriate semantic content; such individuals are also found to use few iconic gestures. In Broca's aphasia there is appropriate semantic content but little overall structure or fluency and iconic gestures are preserved.

Iconic gestures are not separate from thinking and speech but part of it. Potentially they allow us an enormous insight into the way people think because they offer an insight into thinking through a completely different medium from that of language; a medium that is imagistic rather than verbal. Such gestures may indeed offer a window into the human mind and how it represents our thinking about events in the world. It may also tell us, through an analysis of the degree of temporal asynchrony of the gesture and accompanying speech, which utterances are really spontaneous and which are being deliberately sent for effect. Politicians who want to be well prepared in terms of the delivery of their message and in total control at all times, and yet at the same time want to look informal and spontaneous, might like to take note at this point.

Metaphoric gestures

The second type of gesture is called a *metaphoric* gesture. These are similar to iconic gestures in that they are essentially pictorial, but the content depicted here is an abstract idea rather than a concrete object or event. In the words of David McNeill: 'The gesture presents an image of the invisible – an image of an abstraction.' McNeill (1992: 14) uses the following example to illustrate the concept of a metaphoric gesture:

It [was a Sylves]ter and Tweety cartoon
Metaphoric: Hands rise up and offer listener an 'object'.

According to McNeill here the speaker makes the genre of the cartoon, which is an abstract concept, concrete in the form of a gestural image of a bounded object supported in the hands and presented to the listener. In McNeill's words 'the gesture creates and displays this object and places it into an act of offering'. Borrowing the terminology of the late I. A. Richards (1936) on the nature of metaphor, McNeill argues that the *topic* of the metaphor, the abstract concept that the metaphor is presenting, is the genre of the story (a cartoon) and the *vehicle* of the metaphor, the gestural image, is a bounded, supportable, spatially localizable physical object. The *ground* here, the common ground of meaning on which the vehicle and topic are linked, is that genres of story, meaning and knowledge are like physical containers with physical properties (evidence for this is also found in language itself with expressions such as 'a deep understanding', 'shallow insight', 'broad knowledge', etc.).

Here are a couple of examples of metaphoric gestures from my own corpus. 'Blue' is an English pop group that was appearing on the *Lorraine Kelly Show* on Sky Television. They were discussing with Lorraine Kelly when the band would be touring again. Lee is one of the members of the band.

LEE: For us it's like [we was there] last year

Metaphoric: fingers on left hand curled up, but thumb is stretched out. Hand moves upwards in front of left-hand side of chest and thumb points towards the top of the left shoulder.

This is a metaphoric gesture, the *topic* being the abstract concept, which is time, the *vehicle* being the gestural image, which critically involves the use of the gestural space around the body, and the *ground* is that the future can be thought of as the area in front of the body and the past as the area behind the body.

Here is another example from my corpus. The Appleton sisters are celebrities in Britain and were at one time part of the group All Saints. They are being interviewed on television in a public location. Nicole is describing how she got her figure back so quickly after having a baby.

NICOLE: Working, moving house and lots of stress. It works. It's the [new diet].

Metaphoric: fingers on right hand are straight and slightly apart, hand rises to a position next to the right-hand side of the face. Hand rotates slightly to its left and then to its right three times.

A 'diet' can be a fairly abstract concept. Some diets involve cutting down on food or eating only certain types of food; others involve graded exercise in conjunction with restrictions on eating. Few diets involve just the stresses associated with work and moving house. In this metaphoric gesture, Nicole makes the abstract concept of a 'diet' quite concrete, she is saying that this was a diet based primarily on activity rather than food intake, and it was a particular type of activity – repetitive, constant and vigorous, all depicted in the metaphoric gesture.

The beat

The third main type of gesture is the *beat*. These are movements that look as if they are beating out musical time. Beats tend to have the same form regardless of the content of the speech that they are accompanying. The typical beat, according to McNeill, is the 'simple flick of the hand or fingers up and down, or back and forth; the movement is short and quick and the space [in which the gesture is made] may be the periphery of the gesture space (the lap, an armrest of the chair etc.)' (1992: 15). Beats look like the most insignificant of all gestures but the simplicity of their form belies their real importance. They accompany the most significant parts of the speech, not necessarily particular words, which are important merely because of their content, but the most significant words in the discourse from the speaker's point of view. Thus, even beats with their regular and simple form may provide a clue as to the inner workings of the mind of the speaker. They demarcate those parts of the discourse that speakers themselves consider most significant, regardless of what anybody else might think.

Different vehicles of meaning 6

David McNeill argues that the method by which gestures convey meaning is fundamentally different to the way language does this. Language acts by segmenting meaning so that an instantaneous thought is divided up into its component parts and strung out through time. Consider the following example from my own corpus, which again derives from someone telling a cartoon story:

the table can be [raised up towards the ceiling]
Iconic: hands are resting on knee; hands move upwards, palms pointing down, forming a large gesture, hands continue moving until the hands reach the area just above shoulder level.

The single event here is being described both by language and by the accompanying iconic gesture. The speech does this in a linear and segmented fashion, first identifying what is being raised ('the table') and then describing the action ('can be raised up') and then describing the direction of the action ('towards the ceiling'). The linguist de Saussure (1916) argued that this linear-segmented character of language arises because language is essentially one-dimensional whereas meaning is essentially multi-dimensional. Language can only vary along the single dimension of time with regard to the units out of which it is comprised. As the psychologist Susan Goldin-Meadow and her colleagues note in 1996: 'This restriction forces language to break meaning complexes into segments and to reconstruct multidimensional meanings by combining the segments in time.' But the gestures that accompany language do not convey meaning in a linear and segmented manner; rather they can convey a number of aspects of meaning at the same time in a single multidimensional gesture. The gesture above depicts the table (and its size), and the movement (and its speed), and the direction of the movement, all simultaneously. The important point is that, as Goldin-Meadow notes, the iconic gestures which accompany speech 'are themselves free to vary on dimensions of space, time, form, trajectory, and so forth and can present meaning complexes without undergoing segmentation or linearization'.

According to David McNeill (1992) gestures are also different from speech in terms of how they convey meaning. Speech relies on 'bottom-up' processing, in that the meanings of the words are combined to create the meaning of the sentence. To understand a sentence you have to start with the lower level words (hence 'bottom-up'), whereas in gestures we start with the overall concept portrayed by the gesture. It is this concept which gives rise to the meaning of the individual parts (hence 'top-down'). McNeill provides the following example:

> The gesture is a symbol in that it represents something other than itself – the hand is not a hand but a character, the movement is not a hand in motion but the character in motion, the space is not the physical space of the narrator but a narrative space, the wiggling fingers are not fingers but running feet. The gesture is thus a symbol, but the symbol is of a fundamentally different type from the symbols of speech.
>
> This gesture–symbol is global in that the whole is not composed out of separately meaningful parts. Rather, the parts gain meaning because of the meaning of the whole. The wiggling fingers mean running only because we know that the gesture, as a whole, depicts someone running.
>
> (McNeill 1992: 20)

The important point to remember here is that when produced by this same speaker, this wiggling finger gesture may well have a different meaning (McNeill points out, for example, that it was also used for 'indecision between two alternatives'). In order to argue that gestures are processed like language in a bottom-up fashion, you would need to be able to demonstrate that the three components which comprise the running gesture – the V hand shape, the wiggling motion and the forward movement – have relatively stable meanings in the person's communicational repertoire, which can be recognized and interpreted wherever they are used. But this is not the case.

Another important difference between speech and gesture is that different gestures do not combine together to form more complex gestures:

> With gestures, each symbol is a complete expression of meaning unto itself. Most of the time gestures are one to a clause but occasionally more than one gesture occurs within a single clause. Even then the several gestures don't combine into a more complex gesture. Each gesture depicts the content from a different angle, bringing out a different aspect or temporal phase, and each is a complete expression of meaning by itself.
>
> (McNeill 1992: 21)

Gestures also convey meaning in a different way because there are no standards of form with gestures. Standards of form are a defining feature of all languages. All linguistic systems have standards of well-formedness to which all utterances that fall within it must conform, or be dismissed as not proper or not grammatical. Gestures have no such standards of form. Thus, different speakers display the same meaning in idiosyncratic but nevertheless recognizable ways. As McNeill (1992: 41) says: 'Lacking standards of form, individuals create their own gesture symbols for the same event, each incorporating a core meaning but adding details that seem salient, and these are different from speaker to speaker.' This non-standardization of form is very important for theoretical reasons: 'Precisely because gestures are not obliged to meet standards of form, they are free to present just those aspects of meaning that are relevant and salient to the speaker and leave out aspects that language may require but are not relevant to the situation' (1992: 22).

In the example below from my corpus, which has been chosen because of its obvious simplicity, each of the three speakers creates the spinning movement of the table, but they do this differently. One uses one finger, two use both arms, two use clockwise movements, one makes an anti-clockwise movement, two make two movements, one makes three movements (Beattie and Shovelton 2002a). The point of this particular picture in the cartoon story is to show the chaos caused when Billy gets on a chair that now spins causing a table to spin. One of the gestures seems to focus specifically on the rapid speed of the spinning; one specifically on the extent of the spinning; and the third depicts both aspects simultaneously.

Actual speech and gestures produced by three different narrators	Event referred to
[It like spins round] *Iconic: left index finger makes three rapid, small clockwise movements.*	
The table went [spinning] *Iconic: right arm moves in two large clockwise circles, while the left hand moves away from and then towards the right arm.*	Billy Whizz causes a table to spin around
Wrecks everything [spinning round and round and round and round and round] *Iconic: both arms make two large rapid anti-clockwise movements.*	

This is one major difference between the kinds of iconic gestures that we are discussing here and the sign languages of the deaf. The gestural languages of the deaf have the same fundamental properties as verbal language and are quite different from the spontaneous iconic gestures that people create while they are talking. Sign languages have to be able to split complex meanings into their component parts and then to reconstitute the meaning through combinations of signs. This necessitates a lexicon and therefore standards of well-formedness and a syntax, or a set of rules for combining signs that includes word order, to form meaningful sentences. The gestures that accompany speech have no such lexicon and no such syntax.

The iconic gestures that accompany speech also depend upon their iconicity to convey meaning. The gesture as a whole spontaneously created by the individual in conversation must be a good representation of the thing to which it is referring. The movements of the fingers or hands described above are obviously a good iconic representation of the concept of spinning. If something that is being depicted is moving very slowly, the spontaneous iconic gesture that is depicting it must also be very slow. This is different from sign languages, where in American Sign Language the sign for 'very slow' is the sign for 'slow' made more rapidly. This speeding up of the sign is quite arbitrary, and quite unlike what happens with spontaneous iconic gestures, which are not arbitrary in this way. This dimension of arbitrariness (discussed by Hockett and others) found in sign languages is what, of course, characterizes ordinary verbal language. In ordinary verbal language we don't assume that 'head' and 'lead' or 'hedge' and 'ledge' will be similar in meaning. As Shakespeare wrote:

> What's in a name? that which we call a rose
> By any other name would smell as sweet

The point that Shakespeare is making is that the concept of rose could quite well be called something else. The name is arbitrary. But this is not the case for the spontaneous iconic gestures that accompany speech. These would have to represent a rose in a non-arbitrary way; perhaps by illustrating the bloom (hands opening to form a circular shape); perhaps illustrating the thorns on the stem (hands iconically portraying the sharp inverted 'V' shape of the thorn); or perhaps even depicting the expression of a lover presented with one (hands opening with awe and gratitude).

Therefore, iconic gestures and speech convey meaning in radically different ways, with speech relying on a lexicon for breaking meaning down into its component parts and a syntax for combining these various elements into meaningful sentences, whereas iconic gestures represent multidimensional meanings simultaneously in one complex image. Each speaker creates the iconic gestures spontaneously without relying on a lexicon with defined standards of form, and even consecutive iconic gestures do not combine into higher order units. Each gesture is complete in itself, and the overall meaning of what is being portrayed gives the meaning to the individual components. It is also important to emphasize that the meaning in the gesture may, on occasion, never be represented in the speech itself and thus may carry powerful new information about what the speaker is thinking.

McNeill also suggests that 'the gestures of people speaking different languages are no more different than the gestures of different people speaking the same language. While their speech moves in different directions to meet linguistic standards, their gestures remain close together'. This is an extraordinary suggestion because when we think of the gestures of people who speak different languages we think of difference and diversity; we think of the extravagant gesticulations of the Italian compared to the rather more inhibited gesticulation of the English. Indeed, it has been recognised since the 17th century that those from southern Italy make more use of the hands when talking than those from northern Europe, but that both the frequency and form of the gestures change with cultural assimilation. The classic study into the effects of cultural assimilation on gestures was carried out by David Efron during the 1930s in New York City. He found that both the number and type of gestures used by assimilated eastern Jews and assimilated southern Italians differed greatly from their traditional cultures and had started resembling each other. His research emphasized both cultural differences in gesture and the effects of the intermingling of different cultures on the nature of the gestures used (1941/1972). Others have focused on cultural differences in gesture and this process of cultural assimilation in different languages and cultures. In describing Arabic gesture, Robert Barakat writes:

> Arabs . . . make extensive use of a vast variety of gestures and body movements to register reactions to events and peoples, or to communicate messages silently . . . the Arab is often accused of speaking with his hands and body as well as his mouth. So intimately related are speech, gesture and culture, that to tie an Arab's hands while he is speaking is tantamount to tying his tongue.
> (Barakat 1973: 751)

Barakat also outlines how Arabic gestures change with the process of cultural assimilation in that Arab students living in the USA attempt to inhibit some of the more conscious gestures that would normally be interpreted as peculiarly Arabic. Gestures, for example, that involve bodily contact between males, which would be perfectly acceptable in Arabic culture but taboo in western cultures, tend to be inhibited. When we think of people speaking different languages we tend to be aware of how different the gestures are, while sometimes recognizing the influence of cultural assimilation on the process. We also think of how emblems, those gestures which are used consciously and intentionally to replace speech, can be misunderstood in different places; the palm-back and the palm-front V signs mean quite different things in the UK, whereas in the rest of Europe they have exactly the same meaning, that of 'victory'. Although interestingly I do have a photograph of Mrs

Thatcher from the early 1980s giving the palm-back V sign to a group of devoted Tory supporters, the particular smile on her face makes this an unusual photograph in many respects.

According to the theory that is being discussed here, differences in gesture use (excluding emblems, of course) in different languages and in different cultures are relatively trivial compared to the underlying similarities in their use.

I explored this in a study with a PhD student, Rima Aboudan, in which we asked native Arabic speakers to narrate the same basic cartoons used with our English speakers (see Aboudan & Beattie 1996). One story concerned a ghostly, disembodied hand starting an old-fashioned car with a starting handle while the owner, an upper-class elderly man in tweeds and a bow tie, was trying to push it to get it started. In other words, the ghostly hand was helping the elderly man out. One English-speaking narrator used the following speech–gesture combination*:

* Here we are interested in the whole gesture and not just the stroke phase, so the brackets indicate the boundaries of the whole gesture. This also applies to all the examples in the rest of this chapter and in Chapter 7.

so [the hand is now trying to start the car]
Iconic: hand forms a fist and performs four circular movements in front of body.

Another said the following with the accompanying gesture:

[starting it at the front with the] winder thing
Iconic: hand forms a fist and performs four circular movements in front of body.

One Arabic speaker with a particular Syrian dialect, on the other hand, used the following speech–gesture combination to refer to the same event:

تشغّلو السيارة، يظهر على الموديل القديم [بالمانيول هاندل]

The idiomatic English translation of this Arabic sentence is:

<u>Trying to start the car in an old-fashioned way by using [a manual handle]</u>
Iconic: hand forms a fist and performs three circular movements in front of body.

The similarities were striking from speakers from two different cultures which use very different languages. In each of the three examples, exactly the same gesture was used with almost identical preparation, stroke and retraction phases. Even the basic timings were similar. The first English speaker had a preparation phase during which the fist was formed of 200 milliseconds, followed by a stroke phase during which the winding movements were performed of 1320 milliseconds, followed by a retraction phase where the fingers of the fist uncurled of 280 milliseconds. The second English speaker displayed essentially the same movements in a preparation phase of 120 milliseconds, followed by a stroke phase of 1080 milliseconds, followed by a retraction phase of 360 milliseconds.

The Arabic speaker again performed the same movements in a preparation phase of 160 milliseconds, followed by a stroke phase of 1000 milliseconds, followed by a retraction phase of 480 milliseconds. The overall duration of the gesture varied from 1560 milliseconds to 1800 milliseconds; both English speakers were at the extremes with the gesture of the Arabic speaker falling somewhere in between. So in approximately one and a half seconds of animated talk, an Arabic speaker and a number of English speakers demonstrated some striking similarities in the types of unconscious iconic gesture they were generating alongside their speech.

There were some interesting differences in the speech used. The speech of the Arabic speaker seems to be the most explicit, leaving least for the gesture to communicate. The speech here made it clear that the car was being started in 'an old-fashioned way' and that 'a manual handle' was being used. But nevertheless the gesture still showed exactly how the manual handle was used. The speech does not after all explicitly state that it was 'a starting handle'; 'a manual handle' is a somewhat vaguer term. Neither of the two English speakers in their speech mentioned how the car was being started. One didn't mention it at all; the other merely stated that 'a winder thing' was being used. The iconic gesture was necessary to show how the car was being started.

There appear to be differences in those parts of speech accompanied by the gestures in the two languages. In the two English examples the gesture accompanies the verb phrase, whereas in Arabic it accompanies a noun phrase. But in other English examples where the speaker is more explicit in terms of the linguistic channel and includes a mention of 'the starting handle', the iconic gesture is found on some occasions to accompany at least part of this noun phrase rather than the verb phrase as in some of the examples provided earlier. For example:

by turning [the starting] handle
Iconic: hand forms a fist and performs five circular movements in front of body.

Another set of examples from the same experiment again demonstrates the close similarities in iconic gesture across different cultures and language groups in how events are represented unconsciously. Here one Arabic-speaking narrator used the following gesture–speech combination to describe how the ghostly hand manages to keep an irate policeman down a manhole:

ضاغطه عليه] بحيث انه ما يقدر يطلع

This translates as:

[pushing him down] so that he cannot get out
Iconic: right hand rises up from rest position with palm facing down, fingers extended, downward motion as if pressing down on something.

One English speaker used the following gesture–speech combination:

the hand is [pushing down] on the policeman's head
Iconic: right hand rises up from rest position with palm facing down, fingers extended, downward motion as if pressing down on something. Repeated twice.

Another English speaker said:

by [pushing down] on his head
Iconic: left hand rises upwards with palm facing down, fingers extended, downward motion as if pressing down on something. Repeated three times.

The gestures in both English and Arabic show how the pushing down was accomplished; i.e. it was done with the hand rather than with anything else, and that the hand had to be extended in order to do this and finally that the palm had to be facing downwards. The iconic gesture also conveyed something about the resistance that the ghostly hand had to overcome in order to keep the policeman in the manhole. In Arabic the verb comes first in the sentence and it was here that the iconic gesture occurred (the Arabic has to be read from right to left). In English, the subject comes before the verb but the gesture accompanied the appropriate action part of the sentence.

The duration of the gesture, including the very similar preparation, stroke and retraction phases were 1360 milliseconds for the Arabic speaker, 1480 milliseconds for the first English speaker and 1720 milliseconds for the second English speaker; less than half a second difference between the longest and the shortest.

These similarities are all the more surprising not just given the focus in the published literature on differences in gesticulation between cultures, although previous research has not focused on the detailed micro-analysis of individual unconscious gestures like those being studied here, but also given the enormous linguistic differences between Arabic and English. The standard sentence structure in English is the subject–verb–object pattern but the standard pattern in Arabic is verb–subject–object. Arabic is also read from right to left, not from left to right. The iconic gesture accompanied the appropriate part of the utterance in the two languages even though the surface forms of the utterances were very different. The similarity of the gestures across languages thus suggests an essential similarity of thought in the development of utterances irrespective of the specific language used (interested readers might like to consult Aboudan and Beattie 1996 for further detail on this point).

To summarize, the fundamental idea here is that the images depicted in the hand gesture and the verbal utterance emerge together from the same underlying idea or representation. It is not that the gesture is a translation of the sentence or an independent visual display simply shown at the same time as the verbal utterance; the real division of meaning between the gesture and the speech argues against that idea, as would the close integration of the various phases of the gesture with the utterance. The fact that gestures convey meaning in a totally different way to speech with its linear segmented nature would suggest that the gesture does not arise from some advanced verbal plan of the utterance but rather that the two forms of communication arise from some underlying primitive idea. Analysis of the iconic gesture allows us potentially a great deal of insight into the nature of that primitive idea.

Gestures and the frustrations of everyday life *7*

Imagine a dinner party where old friends have met to discuss their schooldays. They are sitting around a long oak table lit by candles in silver candlestick holders. Life has been good to them. Each one has been something of a success in life and they are now looking back fondly, the way that you do when you can afford to. One has just told the story of how he was habitually late for school assembly. 'But it never did me any harm,' he says with a slight wry smile, very pleased with himself now that he runs a successful advertising agency. 'Go to work without an egg, eat a snack happy bar instead, nothing inside but pure white sugar' was unfortunately one of his efforts. 'My lateness is seen as a power trip these days; my clients have come to expect it,' he says. 'Lateness is a semiotic extension of power, they know the rules and rituals of everyday life.'

One has been discussing the French teacher, Mr Snowball, whom they used to call Monsieur Bal Neige. 'Well he told us to use French for everything in class,' she explains with a laugh, 'but he hated being called that – Bal Neige, it even sounds revolting.' The third is just about to describe how she flicked some note across the classroom using a protractor, but Monsieur Bal Neige intercepted the note and she was given detention, where she met her future husband, later to become the chief executive of some PR agency. That at least was her intention. There was only one slight problem, however. She couldn't remember the name for that plastic object which measures angles in geometry; that plastic thing which was once so important in her maths class.

She began the story quite successfully. 'Do you remember that French class where I flicked the note across the room with the . . . what's it called, you know, the what's it?' The faces around the table looked at her face encased in a wince. 'Oh God,' she says. 'What's it called?' She taps her foot on the floor repeatedly; she puts both hands up to her head.

'A set square,' the ever-late advertising executive who is deeply into semiotic extension says helpfully.

'No, no, no,' she replies, 'not one of those, the other thing, the what's it?' And at this point we must all step back from the immediacy of her language to consider her body language and particularly her iconic gestures as she tries to find the word.

Oh it's a type of circumference thing, I know what it is, it's that [bloody arc thing. Oh no what's the word] it's on the tip of my tongue. It's
Iconic: right hand makes a semi-circular movement, moving quickly up and downward twice with index finger pointing outwards. Right hand and left hand then move quickly round each other five times in circular fashion.

[erm circumferential]
Iconic: hands move in and out three times touching at fingertips and base of palm in a curved fashion.

[Oh shit excuse me]. It's driving me crazy.
Iconic: right hand makes a semi-circle shape.

[Erm] It's an arc, no it's an arch, it's a ro- something. It's an, oh God, something arc . . . arch . . . rotor . . . arc.
Iconic: right hand makes a semi-circle shape.

'Please won't somebody help me?' she says.

'Is it a protractor?' suggests the tormentor of Monsieur Bal Neige, and a new expression sweeps across the face of the tormented one. She had only meant to tell a brief and amusing story about how chance and fate determine all our lives, and instead she was locked into a frustrating and highly public situation of complete failure where she was unable to locate the right word in her mental dictionary, the failure no doubt occasioned by the fact that she had not used or discussed a protractor since she left school (or even mentioned it in previous versions of the story), plus she had been drinking a lot of *Pinot Noir*.

There are a number of interesting things to comment on here: our response to routine cognitive failures of this type, others' reaction to us, the willingness of others to help us out, a sort of cognitive midwifery, our demands that they should assist us in this way; but the most interesting things in the present context are the iconic hand gestures that are generated during this failure, iconic gestures that seem to map out significant features of the word being searched for, the fact that a protractor is curved, and indeed semi-circular, unlike a set square, which might have seemed like a reasonable alternative.

This example has been made up – the dinner party never occurred, the advertising executive never existed although Mr Snowball did – but the phenomenon, this tip-of-the-tongue state with the accompanying iconic gestures did occur, although the words have been changed slightly to make it more comprehensible. We will see the actual words shortly and learn something of the context in which this tip-of-the-tongue state really did occur. But such occurrences have led some psychologists to argue that this is the real function of iconic gestures, to help us find the words that we are looking for in everyday speech.

Having got thus far in the overall argument it is useful to pause and consider whether iconic gestures could actually have quite a different function to that suggested by David McNeill. Some psychologists have argued that iconic gesture and speech are clearly not separate, which is also the starting point for McNeill's argument. Also if you watch speakers who have difficulty in finding the word that they are looking for in everyday speech, often in their frustration they produce an iconic gesture. This gesture is clearly connected to the word that they are looking for, as if (and this is the critical bit) this gesture might somehow be helping them find the word. Furthermore, those who suffer from aphasia, who have an impairment of language abilities following brain damage, often have word-finding difficulties and appear to gesture more as a result. Could this be the main function of iconic gestures – that is, could iconic gestures really be used by speakers to help them locate words in their mental dictionary, the mental store of intuitive knowledge of words and their meanings? Is this why we gesture so much on the telephone? Even though we know that listeners cannot see our gestures, do we still gesture because we are really using them for our own benefit in our effort to produce meaningful and interesting speech?

This is an intriguing idea. Word finding in everyday speech, access from the mental dictionary in our brains, is something that we tend to take for granted, except when it goes wrong, as in the imaginary dinner party, and fails to happen quite as it should, as in aphasia or when we find ourselves stuck momentarily for a word during routine conversation. Then perhaps for the first time we think of how complicated this process actually is.

The rate of such word finding in speech is very impressive. It has been estimated at between 120 and 250 words per minute on average (Maclay and Osgood 1959), but with bursts of up to twice this rate. The rate during actual articulation (that is ignoring all those unfilled pauses, those brief silent pauses which in the case of speech involving spontaneous thinking can comprise half or even more of all speaking time) is nearer the top end of this estimate rather than the bottom. So just imagine, therefore, how frequently we have to delve into that mental store to pull out the required items to produce coherent and fluent sentences. This is clearly a very rapid process but how complex a task is it really? Well, there are a lot of words in our mental dictionary and also a lot of words to choose from that may be appropriate for any given slot in an utterance. How many words exactly do we have in this mental store? The answer is that nobody really knows. The Dutch psychologist Willem Levelt (1993) has pointed out that there are fairly reliable ways of estimating the size of our word-*recognition* lexicon (for example, showing a sample to people and seeing what proportion they recognize). This word-recognition lexicon has been estimated as consisting of approximately 75,000 items for Oxford undergraduates by Oldfield (1963), but there are no comparable methods for estimating the size of the *production* lexicon, i.e. the words that we actually employ ourselves rather than just recognize. Levelt has suggested that we have around 30,000 words in our production lexicon, but he notes that this estimate could be out by a factor of two, with perhaps as many as 60,000 words available. So just imagine people in their everyday conversations producing coherent speech, with all the right words in the right places, chosen from all of these alternatives, at this sort of rate. It is also an extremely efficient cognitive skill because we can access this huge database at such high rates, over long stretches of time and without any obvious signs of fatigue. The skill is also characterized by a very low error rate. It has been reported that there were only 86 errors of word choice in a spoken corpus of 200,000 words, with 105 other slips of the tongue.

So just try to imagine this process in action, that is finding the right words at the right time in everyday talk. It's like consulting the *Concise Oxford Dictionary*, which has 75,000 entries, up to four times a second and getting it right almost every time for hours and hours on end.

There have been a number of different approaches by psychologists to the question of how word finding operates in speech. Some researchers have studied natural spontaneous speech, examining where the brief unfilled or silent pauses actually occur. These sometimes reflect the delay in finding certain words and tell us where speakers have most difficulty in accessing certain words or types of word. Unfilled pauses occur before categories of words like nouns and verbs, which have the lowest frequency in the language as a whole.

Iconic gestures have been implicated in the process of word selection for two main reasons. First, the words that iconic gestures are most clearly associated with in everyday speech are nouns and verbs – the main content words that tend to be associated with pauses in speech and seem hardest to access. Second, because the preparation phase of a gesture precedes the associated word, the gesture might be thought to be mapping out some core parts of the meaning of the word, perhaps to help the speaker find the right word in the mental dictionary. In other words, iconic gestures may be involved in (and also able to reveal some of the processes behind) the generation of speech, a process that is otherwise notoriously difficult to study.

Detailed analysis of a small corpus of natural speech taken from a variety of academic interactions, which I carried out as a student at Cambridge, then revealed a strong association between the presence of iconic gestures and particular form classes of words, particularly nouns, verbs and adjectives – the classes which contain the words most difficult to retrieve in speech. These observations led Brian Butterworth and me to the tentative conclusion that certain types of gesture are products of word-finding processes and indicate that speakers know in advance some aspects of the meaning of words before the words them- selves are actually uttered (see Beattie 1983). Brian Butter- worth and Uri Hadar (1989) attempted to develop a model of this process to show why such iconic gestures might assist in this process of locating words in the mental dictionary. They suggested that the visual image in the iconic gesture displays certain core parts of the meaning of the word that is being searched for because 'word finding is delayed by the slow build-up of activation [in the brain] in the searched for word. By raising the overall activation in the system through the production of a motor movement, the word will reach a firing level more quickly'.

In the previous section of this book we saw some examples of different speakers describing the same event from the story 'The Haunts of Headless Harry', where a ghostly hand started an old-fashioned car with a starting handle. What is interesting is that some of the examples from this experiment seem to fit into one theory, that of David McNeill, and other examples fit into the alternative theory, that of Butterworth and Hadar. For example:

<u>so [the hand is now trying to start the car]</u>
Iconic: hand moves in a winding movement.

This first example seems to fit directly into McNeill's theory, which holds that iconic gestures do not assist in word finding; rather they operate in conjunction with the speech itself to communicate the speaker's thinking. In McNeill's words: 'To get the full cognitive representation that the speaker had in mind, both the sentence and the gesture must be taken into account.' In this example, the speech conveys only part of the overall message, the iconic gesture conveys another complementary part, i.e. how the car is actually being started, and to get the full cognitive representation of what the speaker had in mind both the sentence and the gesture must be taken into account. The sentence is also well formed and the iconic gesture is clearly not a repair, or an attempt to fix the sentence in any way. Furthermore, the sentence appears extremely fluent even when the unfilled pauses in speech (as brief as 200 milliseconds) are analysed.

Now consider a second example, which comes from a different speaker narrating the same cartoon:

<u>(pause) [starting it at the front with the (pause)] winder thing</u>
Iconic: hand moves in a winding movement.

Here, the iconic gesture starts and finishes before its associated words ('winder thing'). There are also brief silent pauses in this segment of speech and the gesture starts and terminates in two of these pauses. Here the gesture boundaries include the preparation and retraction phases of the gesture. The speaker does not find 'starting handle' and settles instead for 'the winder thing'. This example, it could be argued, fits more clearly into Butterworth and Hadar's theory and one could imagine a possible role for the iconic gesture in word finding here. The iconic gesture is mapping out the actions involved in using a starting handle and this aspect of its use may help find the location in the brain where the word is actually stored.

In the third example we find more hesitations – both silent and filled ('ah', 'er', 'um', etc. – pauses filled with some sound). Again, there is a gap between the start of the preparation phase of the iconic gesture and the generation of the word with which the gesture is most clearly associated, although the correct word is eventually found in this particular case after a number of pauses.

by (pause) [turning the eh] (pause) <u>starting handle</u>
Iconic: hand moves in a winding movement.

But the problem here is that even such detailed analyses of the precise relationship between speech and iconic gesture cannot really answer the question of the possible functional role of iconic gesture in word finding. Mere associations of this kind cannot prove causality; the results are always going to be too inconclusive. Some examples seem to go along with Butterworth and Hadar's theory, while some do not. Even when they do and it looks as if there is evidence of word-finding difficulty and the iconic gestures precede the word, mapping out some relevant features, then McNeill's theory can still explain the results because he says that people communicate in gesture–speech combinations. If people have trouble in finding a word in the linguistic channel, it would be appropriate for the gesture still to carry information about that word. Where he differs from Butterworth and Hadar is that he would say that iconic gestures should not in any way help us find the word because that is not what they are designed to do.

I reasoned that what we needed to do was to test experimentally the Butterworth and Hadar theory that iconic gestures have a functional role in word finding. So along with Jane Coughlan I asked participants to narrate cartoon stories, as I had done on a number of occasions before, but this time they were asked to repeat their stories to a number of different listeners on a series of consecutive trails. This was done so that there would be a gradual shift from hesitant spontaneous speech to fluent, well-rehearsed speech. This was based on some early research by a psychologist called Frieda Goldman-Eisler (1968), who had discovered that the more times you repeat a story or a sentence, the more fluent it becomes until the pausing starts to level off. To begin with the pauses are all over the place, as the speaker searches the mental dictionary at many different points in the story for difficult words. But once these difficult words have been found (for example, words like 'starting handle' in the type of story that I was using, which is not in everyday use), on the next occasion that the story is told a shorter pause or no pause at all is necessary to retrieve this word. The speaker has already found 'starting handle' in the first telling of the story. Now it can be found quite quickly when the story is told again. After a number of repetitions of the story, the pauses end up being restricted to mainly grammatical junctures; for example, at the ends of sentences, where they occur even when people are reading text and where they are now being used just to segment the story for the listener.

I wanted to use this method because it seemed to me that if Butterworth and Hadar were correct that iconic gestures are mainly used to help speakers find certain words in the mental dictionary, then you would predict that when words have been found once and used fluently, the possible role of iconic gestures in all subsequent retrieval processes should diminish. Therefore the frequency of iconic gestures should decrease across trials when speakers are telling the same story again and again.

So we asked 8 participants to tell the same story 6 times each, resulting in 48 stories overall. They displayed 694 gestures in total, 403 of which were iconic gestures and 291 were beats. Our results showed that the frequency of iconic gestures did not significantly decrease across trials but rather remained remarkably stable from trial two onwards. By the sixth and final trial, participants were gesturing, on average, 91 per cent as much as they did on the very first trial. Even, for example, when 'starting handle' had been used by participants, whenever they came to use the word subsequently in the repetition of the story, the iconic gesture still occurred, suggesting that whatever the function of the gesture it was not solely being used to generate an image that would help speakers access that part of their mental dictionary where the word was stored (Beattie and Coughlan 1998).

I then tried a different approach to answer this question of whether iconic gestures are primarily concerned with helping us access our mental dictionaries. I used one of the better known experimental techniques, which has been successfully employed to probe other aspects of the mechanism of word finding. The technique involves studying something called the tip-of-the-tongue (TOT) state. The TOT state is a particular type of word-finding problem. If you provide a definition of a word to a set of individuals and they try to give you the word, sometimes they do not know it and are certain that they don't know it; sometimes they tell you the word immediately; sometimes they are sure that they know the word but just cannot say it at that precise moment in time. This can be a very frustrating experience for the individuals concerned, which I am sure everybody recognizes, and is called the tip-of-the-tongue state.

This state can be a very useful phenomenon for the experimental psychologist because here, in the words of Harvard psychologist Roger Brown, 'the mind swims excitingly close to the surface'. As A. S. Brown notes:

> Because word retrieval is usually so rapid, examining, in a temporary 'holding pattern' imposed by the TOT, has the potential to reveal subtleties of normal retrieval functions, similar to how slow-motion photography clarifies the dimensions of a humming-bird's flight.
>
> (Brown 1991: 204)

The study of this phenomenon has a long history in psychology. William James, one of the founders of modern psychology, was also intensely interested in the phenomenon and he describes the tip-of-the-tongue experience in the following terms:

> The state of our consciousness is peculiar. There is a gap therein, but no mere gap. It is a gap that is intensely active. A sort of wraith of the name is in it, beckoning us in a given direction, making us at moments tingle with the sense of our closeness and then, letting us sink back without the longed-for term.
>
> (James 1893: 251)

Diary studies have revealed that tip-of-the-tongue states are really quite common in everyday life. In the tip-of-the-tongue state individuals may know certain things about the word. They may know certain parts of the word like the first letter or they may know a particular syllable in the word. They may even be able to suggest similar sounding words with the same first letter, which makes the whole thing that much more frustrating. As Roger Brown (1966: 274) describes: 'It is like fumbling in a file cabinet for a particular card when you know the approximate, but not the exact, location. You come up with a fistful of cards – all wrong but all obviously out of the right drawer.' The information that they do know about the target word may hold a clue as to how the mental dictionary is organised and accessed.

Roger Brown and David McNeill carried out the first really systematic experimental investigation of the TOT state in 1966 (the same McNeill who later turned his attention to gestures, although he never studied the relationship between iconic gestures and the TOT state). In their laboratory, participants were read definitions of rare words from which they had to recall the target. Brown and McNeill define the TOT experience in the following way: 'If you are unable to think of the word but feel sure that you know it and it is on the verge of coming back to you then you are in a TOT state.' They also felt that there were often visible signs of a TOT state. For example, in 57 out of 360 instances, participants 'would appear to be in a mild torment, something like the brink of a sneeze, and if he found the word his relief was considerable'. In this experiment, they found that participants in the TOT state could often provide the initial letter and number of syllables of the target word, even when they could not retrieve the word itself. Overall, tip-of-the-tongue states were experienced in 13 per cent of retrieval attempts in this study.

In my laboratory we investigated whether permitting participants to use gestures in the TOT state affects the rate at which they resolve the state, and thus whether iconic gestures function effectively in finding words in the mental dictionary. My reasoning was that if gestures are associated with word finding, as some psychologists suggest, then when participants are free to gesture (whether in a TOT state or not), they should be able to find the correct word significantly more frequently than those who have their arms folded and are therefore unable to gesture (assuming comparable vocabulary sizes in two randomly chosen groups). Second, if iconic gestures do have a functional role in finding words in the mental dictionary, then they should be involved significantly more in resolved TOT states, those in which they find the word having been in a TOT state, than unresolved TOT states. After all, participants may resolve more TOT states when they are free to gesture but this may, of course, have nothing to do with the occurrence of iconic gestures per se.

We induced a TOT state by reading participants a set of 25 definitions of target words, for example: 'A man's soft felt hat with an indented crown' – *trilby*; 'A material for starting a fire, such as dry wood or straw' – *kindling*; 'The open main court of a Roman house' – *atrium*. When each definition was read out, the participant was told they would have 30 seconds in which to say the word. If they couldn't immediately recall the word, they were then told to keep thinking and to offer any suggestions they might have. If they didn't say the word after 30 seconds, they were given a cue – the initial letter of the target word – in order to increase the number of TOT states further. Some participants didn't have a TOT state until they were given this first letter. They were then allowed a further 15 seconds to say what the target word was. If they didn't get it in the time, they were told it and we moved on to the next word on the list. Half the participants (totalling 30) were instructed to fold their arms and keep them folded throughout so as to prevent any gesturing, while the rest were left free to gesture.

In this experiment we succeeded in eliciting 112 TOT states (in 1500 trials); the TOT states tended to be accompanied by the following types of behaviour (and these behaviours were important in identifying the TOT state):

1. Verbal statements, like 'Oh, God I know it!' or 'Oh, what are they called?' Our participants also sometimes got the initial letter of the word or said words (or non-words!) similar to the target, e.g. 'quiff' or 'quin' for the target word 'quill'.
2. Certain types of facial expression, such as wincing.
3. Certain types of bodily movement, for example, leaning forward and holding their head in their hands.
4. Characteristic head movements, for example, the head falling back, dropping forward, or turning to the side.
5. Characteristic foot and leg movements, for example, excessive tapping and jigging about.

Below is an example of one female participant in a TOT state. You may recognize the example from earlier at the dinner party. The imaginary dinner party scene was based on this example. The definition that had been read to her was 'a semi-circular instrument for measuring angles on paper'. The participant was a university undergraduate, who had obviously some difficulty in recalling the names of those things that she had kept in her pencil case a few years earlier. Most of the behaviours described above were shown here. She felt extremely frustrated that she couldn't find the word. In the 30 seconds before the first letter was provided, she also generated four iconic gestures plus two self-touching movements and one beat, but only the iconic gestures are included in the transcript below. In other words, word-finding problems are clearly associated with the generation of iconic gestures, but do these iconic gestures actually help us find the words? This is the question that this experiment attempts to answer. But first let us see what she actually did during her TOT state.

Oh ts ts curcumf circumference thing I know what it is it's that [bloody arc thing oh no what's the word] it's on the tip of my tongue ts
Iconic: right hand makes a semi-circular movement, moving quickly up and down twice with index finger pointing outwards. Right hand and left hand then move quickly round each other five times in circular fashion.

[erm circumferential]
Iconic: hands move in and out three times touching at fingertips and base of palm in a curved fashion.

[oh shit excuse me] ts
Iconic: right hand makes a semi-circle shape.

[Erm] arc arch ro ro it is r oh God something arc arch rotor arc
Iconic: right hand makes a semi-circle shape.

don't you really want to give me a clue?

The correct answer, of course, was 'protractor' (anyone who has seen or imagined the iconic gesture should have got that). The iconic gestures that accompanied the TOT state tended to illustrate either the shape of the target word (as in the case of the target word 'protractor' above, and also in the case of target words like 'set square' and 'palette') or the function of the target word, for target words like 'stethoscope', 'trowel' or 'castanets'. Sometimes the iconic gesture illustrated both the function of the target word and its shape, as in the case of words like 'accordion' and 'metronome'.

The first prediction tested in this experiment was that if gestures are associated with word finding, then participants who are free to gesture should be able to find the correct word significantly more frequently than those who have their arms folded. Contrary to prediction, we found that the group with arms folded were the more successful in the recall of words (72.4 per cent compared to 66.8 per cent), although this difference was not statistically significant. Nevertheless, this result is clearly at odds with the theory that using iconic gestures helps us find the words we are looking for.

The second prediction was that if iconic gestures do help us find words in our mental dictionary, then they should be involved significantly more in resolved than unresolved TOT states. This was the critical prediction. Although more TOT states were resolved when participants were free to gesture, iconic gestures were not significantly associated with this resolution: 69.0 per cent of TOT states were resolved when iconic gestures were present and 72.9 per cent when they were absent. Furthermore, the resolution rate for TOT states when participants were free to gesture and iconic gestures were present was not significantly different from the resolution rate for TOT states when participants had their arms folded (Beattie and Coughlan 1999).

In other words, this experimental study failed to find any evidence that iconic gestures actually play a significant role in word finding and therefore goes against the Butterworth and Hadar theory. As I stated earlier, the fact that iconic gestures do occur when speakers have trouble finding words is not incompatible with McNeill's basic theory. He argues that speech and gestures originate from a single process of utterance formation with meaning divided between the two channels. The fact that on occasion there may be a problem in finding a word in the linguistic channel does not interfere with the meaning that is being generated in the gestural channel. He has always maintained that the fact that the preparation phase of the gesture precedes the associated speech is important evidence for the fact that both gesture and speech arise from the same common representation, with the more primitive visual image, depicted in the gesture, arising first.

The evidence from the tip-of-the-tongue experiment and related studies (see Beattie and Shovelton, 2000) greatly weakens one of the most powerful opposing theories to that of McNeill. Iconic gestures are common in everyday speech. They do not seem to assist the speaker in retrieving words from the mental dictionary although they are common when speakers are having word-finding difficulties. They often appear to convey aspects of meaning that are not present in the speech itself. Having carried out the tip-of-the-tongue and related experiments, I therefore turned my attention back to the work of McNeill, whose theory I was now starting to believe provided us with a powerful incentive for studying iconic gestures as a way of seeing how the mind really works in everyday life.

Speech is only half the story 8

McNeill's theory of speech and gesture is extremely interesting, but in my opinion it has one fundamental flaw. He never actually demonstrated that listeners extract the information contained within naturally occurring gestures to combine with the information in the speech channel. This is a major shortcoming of a theory that maintains that such gestures are actually *communicative*. All of his analyses are based on whether information appears to be present in the gesture–speech combination. McNeill carried out very few experiments to determine how listeners deal with the information contained within speech and within gestures. He did demonstrate that *staged* gestures and speech that *did not match* in their gesture–speech combinations were combined by listeners in their memory of the event. For example, in the case of a narrator describing a Sylvester and Tweety cartoon who said 'and he came out the pipe', performing an up-and-down bouncing gestural movement at the same time, their utterance was recalled by listeners as the character emerging from the pipe in a particular bouncing manner. McNeill also argued that this process of resolution was done quite unconsciously by listeners and occurred with mismatches of 'form' like the above and 'space', where a particular space identifies one character but the narrator suddenly changes the space in the mismatch in his or her story.

But this experiment was based solely on staged combinations. How do listeners deal with information in the gestural and linguistic channels when they occur naturally? There might be a variety of both theoretical and practical reasons why listeners are unable to use the information from both natural sources. They may not, for example, be attuned to the gesture, except when there is a mismatch. The information contained within the natural gesture might be too vague or too hard to interpret, or listeners might be overcome by the sheer complexity of combining information from linguistic and non-linguistic sources.

A number of other psychologists had attempted to determine if iconic gestures were communicative, but they had all used similar and, in my opinion, unsuitable methods. For example, Krauss, Morrel-Samuels and Colasante (1991) tried to see if people could match gestures with the words that they accompanied and concluded that the relationship between gesture and speech is relatively imprecise and unreliable. However, the Krauss *et al.* study only investigated semantic relationships between speech and gesture, the semantic relationships between the two channels of communication. There were no questions designed to ask about the relationship between gestures and the 'world out there'.

Another experiment that again considered only the semantic relationships between speech and gesture was conducted by Hadar. Here participants had to choose, in a forced choice condition, that word which best described the meaning of a gesture clip shown to them. Hadar concluded that 'although the shaping of gestures is clearly related to the conceptual and semantic aspects of the accompanying speech, gestures cannot be interpreted well by naive listeners' (2001: 294).

It could be argued, however, that this type of approach is in principle unable to answer the question as to the possible communicational function of gestures. If gestures are designed to communicate then they should provide critical information about the semantic domain to be encoded, the world out there or that part of it involved in the experiment, rather than about the accompanying speech.

In a series of studies conducted with Heather Shovelton we decided to tackle this issue. In our first study (Beattie and Shovelton 1999a; see also 1998) we video-recorded participants narrating cartoon stories and then played just the speech segments or the gesture–speech combinations to another set of participants whom we subsequently questioned about details of the original stories. For example, some participants just heard:

Billy going sliding along and causing all sorts of mayhem

The other set of participants were presented with the following gesture–speech combination:

Billy going [sliding along] and causing all sorts of mayhem
Iconic: left hand moves upwards to position in front of chest (preparation phase). Fingers of left hand are straight and close together, palm is pointing downwards. Hand makes a rapid movement to the left (stroke phase in brackets above) then returns to original position (retraction phase).

In this experiment, we studied 34 iconic gestures and 60 participants – 30 participants just heard the speech segments, another 30 were presented with the gesture–speech combinations. After each extract was presented the participant was asked (via a questionnaire) two questions relating to what was happening in the original cartoon. We generated the questions on the basis of what we as the experimenters thought might be being depicted in the gesture. For example, in the extract above we thought that the iconic gesture could have told the listener something about the direction of movement and perhaps also something about the speed of the movement. So we asked two very straightforward questions after each extract was presented. The questions were to be answered by a simple 'yes' or 'no' to make the scoring easy and unambiguous:

'Does Billy slide to his left?'
'Does Billy slide slowly?'

The questions were different for each and every gesture. We asked things like: 'Does the table move in a circular motion as it is rising?' 'Does the boy spin around in a clockwise direction?' 'Is the net very low down?' 'Is the pole very large in relation to the table?' Of these questions 31 related primarily to properties of actions and 37 related to properties of objects. They covered such things as the identity of any people or objects that were talked about, the size of the people or objects, the shape of the people or objects, the number of people or objects discussed, the relative position of the people and objects, the nature of the action in the extract, the speed of any action, the direction of any action and whether the action involved upward movement, rotation or contact, plus we enquired about the location of any action.

The highest possible mean score for each participant for each gesture was 2.00 corresponding to getting both questions correct; the chance probability in answering two yes/ no questions correctly was of course 1.00. We found that those participants who were presented with the gesture–speech combinations got an average of 1.67 questions correct, whereas those who heard only the speech extracts got 1.42 questions correct. The percentage correct in each case was 83.5 per cent and 71.0 per cent respectively. In other words this study demonstrated that those participants who were presented with gesture–speech combinations got significantly more information about the original story than those who only heard the speech. This was an important discovery.

At first sight in purely quantitative terms, this might not seem like much of a difference – an overall increase from 1.42 to 1.67 out of a possible 2.00, but there is something very important which must be considered here. This study was based on yes/no questions, the chance probability where a participant got absolutely no information from the speech or the gesture–speech combination was 1.00, which represents 50 per cent of 2.00. From the speech alone participants got an additional 0.42 units of information, and from the gesture–speech combinations they received an additional 0.67 units of information. Therefore, from the gesture–speech combinations they received 0.25/0.42 more information, which as a percentage is approximately 60 per cent more information. These iconic gestures, in other words, are crucial to the overall message and in purely quantitative terms carry over half as much again as the verbal part of the message. Some individual gestures were found to be even more communicative and indeed carry up to 400 per cent more information.

The iconic gestures also seem to carry information about a whole raft of things, including the speed and direction of the action, whether the action involved rotation or upward movement or not, the relative position of the people and objects depicted, the size and shape of the people and the objects depicted. Clearly these results were very much in line with McNeill's basic theory: if you want to get the full meaning behind a communication you need to take both the iconic gesture and the speech into consideration. Those who either fail to notice or ignore the iconic gestures are clearly missing a source of much potential information.

The next study (Beattie and Shovelton 1999b) tried to be more precise about exactly what information listeners pick up from the iconic gestures that accompany speech. The first study only asked two questions about each iconic gesture, but there was always the possibility that each iconic gesture contained a good deal more information than we were measuring. So in this second study, after each participant heard just the speech or saw just the iconic gesture on its own or was presented with the gesture–speech combination, we asked 8 general questions that we felt explored the 14 relevant types of information with which the iconic gestures were associated:

1. What object(s) are identified here? (*identity*)
2. What are the object(s) doing? (*description of action, manner*)
3. What shape are the object(s)? (*shape*)
4. How big are each of the object(s) identified? (*size*)
5. Are any object(s) moving? (*movement*)
6. If so in what direction are they moving? (*direction, rotation, upward movement*)

7. At what speed are they moving? (*speed*)
8. What is the position of the [moving/stationary] object(s) relative to something else? (*relative position, location of action, orientation, contact*)

Participants in this experiment were presented with 18 clips (six containing only speech, six containing only iconic gestures, and six containing gesture–speech combinations). After the clip was played the interviewer asked the participant half of the questions. The same clip was then played again, and the remaining questions were asked to see what information about the original cartoon they had managed to glean. These interviews, it should be added, were very intensive and lasted up to two hours. Each participant also had to give a confidence rating on each of their judgements on a scale from 1 to 3, where 1 meant 'not confident', 2 meant 'moderately confident' and 3 meant 'very confident'.

The experiment showed that when participants were presented with the gesture–speech combination they were significantly better at answering questions about the original cartoon story than when they heard just the speech extracts. The speech on its own, perhaps not that surprisingly, was significantly better than the iconic gestures on their own. We estimated the mean percentage accuracy for the gesture–speech combinations to be 62.1 per cent, for the speech only to be 51.3 per cent and for the iconic gestures only to be 20.4 per cent (averaging across all of the different categories).

The estimate of how much the iconic gesture adds to the speech is much lower here because all semantic dimensions were considered for every iconic gesture (and we cannot consider the chance probability in the way that we did in the first study). Nevertheless, critical information was clearly carried by the gestures. Even when the iconic gestures are presented in isolation from speech, they still convey a great deal of important information.

There is another very important observation in this study. McNeill had always argued that iconic gestures convey meaning in a 'top-down' rather than a 'bottom-up' fashion;

that is you have to have some understanding of the overall image portrayed in the hand movement before you can understand what the component actions are representing. McNeill says that the individual parts of iconic gestures only convey meaning 'because of the meaning of the whole'. He says: 'The wiggling fingers mean running only because we know that the gesture as a whole depicts someone running.' But this experiment means that we have to add an important proviso to this statement. We found that an iconic gesture can convey the speed of movement, the direction of movement, and also information about the size of the entity depicted in the gesture, even when people watching the iconic gesture in isolation could not determine exactly what the entity actually was. You only had to know that something was sliding along in a particular direction and at a certain speed to get certain questions correct, but you didn't have to be able to say with any confidence what that something actually was. So iconic gestures may operate in a 'top-down' fashion, but that does not mean that you have to get the full meaning at the highest level before any information is transmitted via the gesture. The meaning of the gesture is still global, with the meaning of the individual parts given their meaning by the meaning of the gesture as a whole, but the process can operate even when there is some ambiguity at the highest level.

One of the most extraordinary results in this experiment emerges when you consider the performance of individual participants. Although all the participants gleaned some additional meaning from the iconic gestures, the percentage increase in accuracy in moving from the speech only to the gesture–speech combinations ranged from 0.9 per cent to 27.6 per cent. In fact the analysis also revealed that the participant with the lowest percentage increase in accuracy in moving from the speech only to the gesture–speech combination was also very poor at obtaining information from the iconic gestures on their own, whereas the participant who showed the highest increase in accuracy going from speech only to gesture–speech combinations was very good at obtaining information from the iconic gestures on their own. There was, in fact, a statistically significant correlation between these two things. In other words those participants who obtained most information about aspects of the original cartoon depicted in the clips in the iconic gestures also tended to get the most *additional* information when they saw the iconic gestures in addition to hearing the speech. Clearly some people are neglecting this very important channel of iconic gesture in their everyday life and are therefore missing out on a lot of important information that is clearly available, but is not being picked up by them.

Below are the responses of two participants who watched the same iconic gesture but did not hear the corresponding segment of speech. The first participant, who happened to be male, was good at picking up information from iconic gestures generally and obtained an overall accuracy score of 75 per cent for this particular gesture. The second participant, a female, despite trying very hard, did not display much evidence of having obtained significant amounts of information from iconic gestures generally. In this particular case, she obtained an overall accuracy score of 12.5 per cent.

[Bubbles start coming out of her mouth]
Iconic: Fingers on left hand are spread out and hand moves backwards and forwards in front of mouth.

Example 1, the male participant

> EXPERIMENTER [E]: Do you know what object or objects are identified there?
> PARTICIPANT [P]: It looks as if someone has eaten something hot and steam is coming out of their mouth. So I think I'll say 'steam'.
> E: And how confident are you about that?
> P: Not very – I'll go with two.
> E: So what's being done with it or what's it doing?
> P: I think it is coming out of someone's mouth.
> E: How confident are you about that?
> P: Two again.

E: Do you know what shape the object is?
P: Kind of longish – like steam is. It's really difficult to describe what shape steam is, isn't it?
E: Yeah. So how confident are you there?
P: One.

Clip is then played for the second time.

E: Do you know how big the object is?
P: Well it starts off being small enough to come out of someone's mouth. It might get a bit bigger after, but I'll stick with small.
E: How confident are you about that?
P: One.
E: And is this object moving?
P: Yes. My confidence is three.
E: In what direction and at what speed is it moving?
P: The steam would probably be moving slightly upwards and it would be moving quite quickly. My confidence for both of those is only one.
E: So what do you think the position of the object is, relative to anything else?
P: I think it is moving away from someone's mouth.
E: How confident are you about that?
P: Two.

Example 2, the female participant

E: Have you any idea what object or objects are identified there?
P: A hot drink.
E: OK. And how confident are you about that?
P: Two.
E: And what's being done with it or what's it doing?
P: Kind of waving it, someone is waving it, to make it cool down.
E: How confident are you?
P: One.
E: Do you know what shape the object is?
P: Well, it's in a mug, so the liquid is mug shaped. Yeah.

E: How confident are you about that?
P: Two.

Clip is then played for the second time.

E: OK. Do you know how big the object is?
P: Smallish. Normal mug type size. Confident – two.
E: OK. Is the object moving?
P: No.
E: How confident are you?
P: Three.
E: Do you know what the position of the object is, relative to anything else?
P: It's in someone's hands, on their knee.
E: How confident are you?
P: Three.

This experiment using this interview technique managed to uncover the kinds of information that participants retrieve from iconic gestures, both in isolation from speech and when they are working alongside speech. Let's begin by looking at the clip below:

[she's eating the food]
Iconic: fingers on left hand are close together, palm is facing body, and thumb is directly behind index finger. Hand moves from waist level towards mouth.

Using McNeill's general line of argument, you would probably say that the sentence conveys the action involved ('eating'), but not how it is accomplished. The iconic gesture is critical to communication here because it shows the method of eating – bringing the food to the mouth with the hand. McNeill would also presumably point out that the sentence in the example above is well formed and therefore the gesture cannot be considered as a repair or some other transformation of the sentence. The speech and gesture appear to co-operate to present a single cognitive representation.

Unlike McNeill, we determined, through interviewing three sets of participants who either saw the gesture with or without speech, or did not see the gesture but just heard the speech, what information they *actually* received from the iconic gesture. What we discovered was that they received a wider range of additional information than McNeill's typical argument would suggest. For example, in this particular case all four participants who saw the iconic gesture, in addition to hearing the speech, knew that the food was moving towards the mouth (*relative position*) in the original cartoon, whereas only one out of three participants who did not see the gesture reported this. The other two thought that the food was 'below the character', presumably on a plate. Without hearing the speech (gesture only), one out of three participants got the *description of action* right. All four participants in the video condition (gesture–speech combination) got the *direction* of the movement correct – food was being drawn upwards towards the mouth (only one out of three participants in the speech only condition got this right). None of the participants in the video condition (gesture–speech combination) or the speech only condition got the *shape* of the food correct. The correct answer here, by the way, was a triangular sandwich shape (either triangular or sandwich shaped would have been considered sufficient in the scoring). Very interestingly, one participant in the gesture-only condition said the food was sandwich shaped. With only one participant, of course, it might have been a lucky guess, but since there are so many possibilities here, it was really some guess.

Consider now a second example:

[by squeezing his nose]
Iconic: fingers on left hand are quite straight and only slightly apart; thumb is pointing away from the fingers. Fingers and thumb then move further away from each other before moving towards each other so that hand becomes closed.

Here the sentence conveys the action involved ('squeezing') and the object involved ('nose') and in both the video condition (gesture–speech combination) and the speech-only condition all participants reported this information correctly. However, the gesture seemed to convey information about the *shape* of the nose (oblong shaped) being squeezed. It also conveyed information about the *relative position* of the nose with respect to the hand that is squeezing it and whether the nose was *moving*. The gesture conveyed information about the *size* of the nose and to a much lesser extent the *speed* of the movement.

On the basis of these and similar examples, it could be argued that McNeill had, if anything, underestimated the amount and nature of information conveyed by these seemingly slight and apparently insignificant iconic gestures which accompany everyday speech. Having investigated what information participants actually pick up from such gestures, one can look again at McNeill's examples and analyses, and suggest that even in these examples McNeill was underestimating the full extent of the communication via this gestural channel. Thus, consider again his classic example:

she [chases him out again]
Iconic: hand, gripping an object, swings from left to right.

McNeill argued that the sentence conveys the concepts of pursuit ('chases') and recurrence ('again'), but not the means of pursuit. The iconic gesture, he says, is critical to communication here because it shows the method of pursuit – swinging an umbrella. But one could argue, in the light of this new research (Beattie and Shovelton 1999b), that the gesture here may potentially convey much more information than McNeill allowed for. It may convey other attributes like the *direction* of the swinging (from left to right), the *speed* of the swinging, the *size* of the umbrella and the *relative position* of the umbrella with respect to the hand (vertical, horizontal, etc.). Multiply this example by hundreds of others and it can be seen that there is the possibility that even McNeill may have underestimated the range and types of information conveyed by the iconic gestures which accompany spontaneous speech.

In summary, the experiments that I have just described reveal something of the nature, depth and range of information conveyed by iconic gestures. At one level, it lends considerable support to McNeill's basic idea that such iconic gestures are crucial to meaning. However this study goes beyond this. It not only tells us that such gestures do convey meaning, but it gives the first glimpse of the range of information conveyed by them, and which particular types of information are best captured by them. In this particular study, attributes like the *relative position* of people and objects and the *size* of the people and objects depicted were significant right across the sample of gestures. With respect to these particular types of information it is also interesting to note that it was found that in the gesture-only condition participants were significantly more confident that the answers they were giving were correct than they were when answering questions about *identity, description of action, shape, movement, direction* and *speed*. It is not just that participants were receiving more information in these particular categories right across the board, but they also knew that they were.

These experiments have shown the considerable power of those spontaneous iconic hand gestures that go along with the talk found in everyday life. One question they do not answer is which particular iconic gestures are the most communicative and why. This is the question that we turn to in the next set of experiments where we delve a little deeper into this whole issue.

Who or what the hands portray 9

The experiments described in the previous chapter tell us that iconic gestures convey significant amounts of information, either on their own or combined with speech. David McNeill appears to have been right. But the research described so far does not, of course, mean that every single gesture carries information over and above the speech. Also some iconic gestures appear to carry much more information than others, but what affects this?

There is one absolutely fundamental property of gestures that was not considered in these early studies, but which may well turn out to be critical, because the way that information is depicted in gestures varies greatly depending upon this one property: that is, the *viewpoint* from which the gesture is generated.

McNeill (1992) points out that two different viewpoints appear in the gestures people perform during narratives: observer viewpoint and character viewpoint. A gesture is said to have an observer viewpoint when it appears to display an event from the viewpoint of an observer. McNeill says: 'With this viewpoint, the narrator keeps some distance from the story.' An observer viewpoint gesture 'excludes the speaker's body from the gesture space and his hands play the part of the character as a whole'.

On the next page there is an example of a gesture produced from an observer viewpoint:

[runs out of his house] again
Iconic gesture: thumb of right hand is pointing upwards, other fingers are curled together. Hand moves upwards slightly and then to the right in a rapid movement.

Here the speaker's hand represents the whole cartoon character. The character is in front of the narrator and the character is running, from right to left, but the narrator is not part of the scene.

The other viewpoint that appears when people narrate stories is character viewpoint. Here McNeill (1992) says that with character viewpoint 'we feel that the narrator is inside the story', in that a character viewpoint gesture 'incorporates the speaker's body into the gesture space, and the speaker's hands represent the hands (paws, etc.) of the character'. The running event mentioned earlier could have been conveyed by a gesture produced from a character viewpoint. Thus:

[runs out of his house] again
Iconic: arms bent at elbows, pump backwards and forwards moving from the shoulders.

In this case, the narrator would be moving his arms as if he were actually running himself. The narrator would therefore be imagining himself playing the part of the character rather than external to it, as in the observer viewpoint gesture described earlier.

McNeill's research has suggested that character viewpoint gestures are strongly associated with verbs that take a grammatical object (e.g. 'he hit the ball', where 'ball' is the grammatical object). Observer viewpoint gestures are strongly associated with verbs that do not take an obligatory grammatical object, so-called intransitive verbs (e.g. 'she is jumping', a verb that cannot take a grammatical object, you cannot say 'she is jumping ball', it is quite simply ungrammatical). The viewpoint from which a gesture is generated is a critical variable in the conceptual understanding of gesture and may also have an important influence on the communicative power of individual gestures simply because the hands are being used very differently in these two types of gesture.

Let us have a look at some of the iconic gestures that we have already encountered and consider the viewpoint from which they have been generated so that the distinction becomes completely clear.

<u>and he [bends it way back]</u>
Iconic: hand appears to grip something and pull it from the upper front space back and down near to the shoulder.

This is clearly a character viewpoint gesture. The hands of the speaker act as the hands of the person that he is discussing. The hands show how the object ['the big oak tree' identified in the previous clause] is gripped and pulled back. The clause is transitive; there is a grammatical object, 'it'.

<u>And she [chases him out again]</u>
Iconic: hand appears to swing an object through the air.

This is another character viewpoint gesture. The hands of the speaker are again acting as the hands of the character being discussed. The hands show how the object, 'the umbrella', which is not mentioned in the speech, is being held. This is also a transitive clause with the grammatical object being 'him'.

<u>[she's eating the food]</u>
Iconic: fingers on left hand are close together, palm is facing body, and thumb is directly behind index finger. Hand moves from waist level towards mouth.

Again another character viewpoint gesture – the hands of the speaker are acting as the hands of the character in the story, showing how she eats the food by drawing it up to the mouth. The speech is again another transitive clause with the grammatical object being 'the food'.

<u>the head starts [swimming] along</u>
Iconic: right hand indicates the way that the head is swimming in the water, focusing on forward motion with splayed fingers representing the head.

This one is an observer viewpoint gesture where the hands play the part of the character as a whole, in this case the whole head, which has a life of its own. The speaker takes an observer's perspective on the action; the head is swimming away from the stationary observer, the speaker himself. The speech, in this case, consists of an intransitive clause with no grammatical object. You cannot say 'the head starts swimming it'; it is simply ungrammatical.

But do character viewpoint gestures and observer viewpoint gestures convey different amounts of information, and if so why? How do the hands operate from each of these two different viewpoints? I tested this in another set of experiments (reported in more detail in Beattie and Shovelton 2001a, 2001b, 2002b).

We asked 21 participants to narrate a number of cartoon stories and in this task they displayed a total 513 identifiable hand and arm movements, 103 of which were identified as iconic gestures. Of these gestures 30 were selected for presentation to a set of participants. These 30 gestures were selected on the basis that first the gesture's span did not stretch out of view of the camera and second they depicted different events from the cartoons. There was actually considerable overlap in what the gestures referred to in the cartoon narratives in this particular sample. Of these 30 iconic gestures, 15 were generated from a character viewpoint and 15 from an observer viewpoint.

The speech sample to be played to participants was restricted to the clausal unit in the immediate vicinity of the gesture, again following McNeill's logic that gestures usually do not cross clause boundaries. (However one of the iconic gestures did cross a clause boundary so in this case a slightly larger speech unit was used.) The accompanying 30 speech clauses were then classified regarding their transitivity. Transitive verbs, as I have explained, take obligatory direct objects, intransitive verbs do not take direct objects.

It was found that all of the character viewpoint gestures in our corpus were associated with transitive clauses and all of the observer viewpoint gestures were associated with intransitive clauses. These gestures produced from different viewpoints were randomly ordered onto the presentation tape. Each gesture, without its corresponding speech, was played twice and then the participants had 30 seconds to write down their answer to the following question: 'Please give as much information as possible about any actions and any objects depicted in the following gesture.' We expected the overall accuracy to be lower in this experiment than in the previous study because participants were not interviewed here in the intensive way used earlier.

Again we used eight broad semantic categories to break the meaning down into its parts, namely *identity*, *description of action*, *shape*, *size*, *movement*, *direction*, *speed* and *relative position*, to determine what individual types of information the participants received from gestures.

It is perhaps worthwhile providing a little bit of detail as to how the individual semantic categories were scored in this experiment to illustrate some of the issues involved in this process. After all, if the reader is convinced of the care that went into this process, the final conclusions will seem all that more convincing.

Identity

This semantic category reflects whether or not the participant correctly specified the main entity (person, animal or thing) associated with the iconic gesture. The number of entities contained (or assumed) in each of the clauses varies from one to three. The mean number of entities for intransitive clauses was 1.60 whereas it was 2.27 for transitive clauses. Here is an example of an intransitive clause containing just one entity:

and the [roof starts cracking]
Iconic: index finger of left hand points vertically upwards, other fingers and thumb are slightly curled. Index finger moves to his left and then to his right.

Here the entity is 'roof' and the iconic gesture illustrates the roof cracking.

Below is an example of a transitive clause containing two explicit entities (ball and ground) and one assumed entity (the dog that was actually bouncing the ball):

bouncing the ball [on the ground]
Iconic: palm of right hand points downwards; hand moves rapidly downwards and upwards three times.

Here the gesture mainly illustrates the 'ball' bouncing rather than the nature of the dog doing the bouncing or the nature of the ground on which it is bouncing. We could have attempted to score identity by taking into account all of the entities referred to explicitly or assumed in the linguistic clause but we chose instead to focus on the main entity associated with the iconic gesture, in other words the gesture's principal lexical affiliate ('the ball'). One advantage of scoring it this way was that it allowed for a direct statistical comparison of character viewpoint and observer viewpoint gestures, which do differ in terms of the number of entities in their associated clauses. The alternative strategy would have been to attempt to consider all of the entities in the clause – even those entities that did not appear to be connected to the gesture and indeed those entities that were poorly specified either linguistically or gesturally. We decided that this latter approach was not quite as appropriate.

So the identity category involved the participant correctly specifying the one main entity associated with the iconic gesture. In terms of the categorization, if a participant only used a pronoun in their answer then we reasoned that this did not provide enough information for identity to be scored as correct. For example, if a participant wrote 'he' then this could refer to a number of male entities including a boy, a dog, etc., so for identity to be scored as correct a participant had to specify more precisely what they were referring to. The main entity in five of the clauses was a person or an animal and the other 25 main entities were things like 'a rope', 'a microphone', 'a trolley', 'a pole', 'a nose', 'a tie', etc. In all cases the entity in the participant's answer had to be judged as equivalent in meaning to the specified entity in the clause, before the identity category could be classed as correct.

Shape

This category reflects whether or not the participant correctly specified the shape of the main entity. In the case of one-third of the clips there was only one possible shape for the entity involved and therefore if a participant provided correct information about identity then the shape category was also scored as being correct. For example, bubbles are, by definition, round. Therefore if a participant wrote about bubbles in their answer it could be assumed that they knew that these were round.

In the case of the remaining two-thirds of the clips the shape of the entity had to be explicitly mentioned; for example, a participant would have to explain what shape a table was because it could be a number of different shapes – round, square, etc. Other shapes associated with these clips included 'triangular', 'oblong', 'long and thin', etc.

Size

This category reflects whether or not the participant correctly specified the size of the main entity. Participants had to mention explicitly the correct size of the entity before this category was considered to be correct. The argument that the size of an entity is implicit within the identity category is rejected here because the size of entities in cartoons can vary dramatically. For example, in a cartoon story a 'drink' can be bigger than a boy's body and a 'ball' can contain three kittens but nevertheless fit snugly into a basketball hoop. When the participants' answers were scored any explicit size information that had been provided was placed into the following four categories: 'big', 'medium', 'small', 'varying sizes'.

Movement

This category reflects whether or not the participant correctly specified whether the main entity was moving or not – it was therefore a straightforward dichotomous category. Movement, in this current study, was only scored as correct if there was movement in the original scene and in the participant's answer. In the case of 13.3 per cent of the clips there was no movement, for example 'it's a circular table', and thus this movement category did not apply to these clips.

Description of action

This category reflects whether or not the participant correctly specified what was being done or what was happening in the clip. The description of action in the participant's answer had to be judged as equivalent to the specified action in the clause before the description of action category could be classed as correct. The actions in the clips included 'pushing', 'jumping', 'throwing', etc.

Speed

This category reflects whether or not the participant correctly specified the speed at which the main entity was moving. Again it is important to remember that narrations about cartoons were being analysed – and in cartoon narrations kittens can 'run' so slowly that they never seem to change position with respect to a stationary animal that is giving them instructions. In addition, the kittens can also be watching some action that is happening behind them (very difficult in the case of actual running). In other cartoons, however, characters can 'run' so quickly that they appear to be running faster than a moving car. For this reason it was decided that 'running' alone did not contain implicit speed information but that speed had to be mentioned explicitly. When the participants' answers were scored, any speed information was placed into the following four categories: 'fast', 'medium', 'slow' and 'varying speeds'.

Direction

This category reflects whether or not the participant correctly specified the direction in which the main entity was moving. Again participants had to mention explicitly, rather than implicitly, the correct direction of the movement before this category was considered to be correct. Examples of answers required in the direction category included 'upwards', 'downwards', 'spinning around', etc.

Relative position

This category reflects whether or not the participant correctly specified the position of the main entity with respect to something else. In the present corpus of gestures it seems that there were three major sub-categories contained within the relative position category. First, there was a sub-category that involved the position of the entity with respect to a particular part of another entity and this category contained 15 gestures. An example of relative position information in this category is 'moving away from the mouth'. Next there was a sub-category that involved the position of a moving entity with respect to a fixed entity and this category contained 12 gestures. An example of relative position information in this category is 'moving away from the ground'. The third sub-category involved the position of a fixed entity with respect to another fixed entity and this category contained three gestures. An example of relative position information in this category is 'the bench seat is all the way around something'.

It must also be remembered that for participants merely guessing about the information within each semantic category the chance probability of this guess being correct varied from one category to another. At one extreme was identity and description of action where the chance probability of a correct guess was very low indeed. Next there were the categories of relative position, shape and direction. These were followed by size and speed, where the chance probability was one in four. Finally, at the other end of the scale there was the dichotomous category 'movement'. This was the category that had the highest chance probability of being guessed correctly (50 per cent chance probability).

Two experimenters independently analysed the scenes in the original cartoons, relating to each of the 30 clips, and broke the complex meaning down into the individual categories described above. We then compared these analyses with the answers of the participants who had only seen the iconic gestures produced by our narrators.

Below is an example of one participant's answer. The iconic gesture that was shown to this participant is displayed here with the segment of speech it originally accompanied, which of course was itself not shown in the present experiment:

by [pulling on his tie]
Iconic: left hand moves quickly upwards; hand closes and a sharp downwards movement is made.

After viewing this gesture in the gesture-only condition, one participant wrote: 'Somebody is grabbing hold of a rope with their hand.' In this particular case the gesture was scored as having conveyed information to this participant about the *relative position* of the physical entities involved (i.e. the hand being wrapped around something) and the fact that *movement* was occurring. None of the other semantic categories, namely *identity, shape, size, description of action, speed* or *direction*, were scored as correct in the case of this particular participant, although it should be added that many participants did extract a good deal more information from this particular gesture.

This experiment found that iconic gestures in isolation from speech which were generated from a character viewpoint were significantly more communicative than those generated from an observer viewpoint. The mean accuracy score for gestures generated from a character viewpoint was 18.8 per cent and 10.8 per cent for gestures generated from an observer viewpoint.

Let's look first at the character viewpoint gesture, described above, which had originally been generated accompanying the segment 'by pulling on his tie'. When this iconic gesture was shown to participants in isolation from speech, it conveyed a great deal of semantic information – coded at 18.8 per cent accuracy overall, using the scoring scheme for deconstructing written answers into their underlying semantic categories. This gesture not only provided participants generally with information about the action involved, but also information about the *speed* and *direction of the action* and about the *size* and *shape* of the object involved and the *relative position* of the physical entities depicted in the gesture.

There were, however, still gestures in the present corpus that were generated from an observer's perspective, which were high in communicative power when presented in isolation from speech. For example:

the table can be [raised up towards the ceiling]
Iconic: hands are resting on knee; hands move upwards, palms pointing down, forming a large gesture, hands continue moving until the hands reach the area just above shoulder level. Hands then clasp each other just underneath the chin.

This iconic gesture in isolation communicated significant amounts of semantic information to participants – estimated at 13.5 per cent overall accuracy. This gesture provided participants with information about the action involved (something being raised) along with the *direction of the movement* (upwards). It also provided information about the *size* of the object involved and the *relative position* of the physical entities depicted in the gesture.

When the eight different semantic categories were considered in detail in the analysis, it was found that of the eight individual semantic categories *relative position* was communicated most effectively by character viewpoint gestures in comparison with observer viewpoint gestures. Character viewpoint gestures seem to be particularly good at this semantic category because they can directly show the position of something in relation to the actor's body, the actor's body being central to the generation of a character viewpoint gesture. The actor's body can act as a point of reference, which is not the case with observer viewpoint gestures where the actor's body is necessarily absent. Indeed those character viewpoint gestures in the present study tended to involve relative position information that fell into a particular sub-category of relative position, namely the position of the entity with respect to a particular part of another entity, and character gestures made up 86.6 per cent of this sub-category. Observer viewpoint gestures tended to contain relative position information that fell into the following two sub-categories: the position of a moving entity with respect to a fixed entity (83.3 per cent of these were observer viewpoint gestures); the position of a fixed entity with respect to another fixed entity (100 per cent of these were observer viewpoint gestures).

This experiment demonstrated how a fundamental property of iconic gesture, namely the viewpoint from which it is generated, relates to its communicative power. However, something else was observed in the current study that may have significant implications for our understanding of how iconic gestures work in everyday talk. As mentioned earlier, McNeill (1992) had proposed that character viewpoint gestures tend to be strongly associated with transitive clauses and observer viewpoint gestures with intransitive clauses. In the present corpus we found a perfect association between the transitivity of the clause and the viewpoint of the gesture.

We also found that there was a tendency for the participants to propose transitive structures (e.g. 'he's flicking a coin') in their answers after viewing character viewpoint gestures, and these structures occurred even if the participants could not identity any specific entity involved (e.g. 'he's flicking something' or 'an object is being flicked'). On the other hand, there was a tendency for participants to propose non-transitive answers, either involving intransitive structures or partial answers about the identity of objects (e.g. 'something that is long, thin and smooth') after viewing observer viewpoint gestures. A systematic analysis was therefore carried out of the proportion of answers suggesting a transitive structure for each gesture emanating from a character or from an observer viewpoint. It was found that when participants were watching character viewpoint gestures they were significantly more likely to generate a transitive answer than when they were watching observer viewpoint gestures. This result suggests that character viewpoint gestures not only convey significant semantic information (particularly about the relative position and somewhat less reliably the size of the actual entities involved in the event described) but also about the syntactic structure of the clause. The transitivity of the clause in the linguistic channel, in other words, seems to be partially signalled by the accompanying iconic gesture.

This discovery hints at the complex integration between language and that form of nonverbal communication studied here, namely the movement of the hands during talk. It suggests that the claim that verbal language and bodily movement are separate languages is wrong, at least as far as the movements of the hands are concerned. The nature of the gesture accompanying speech seems to tell the listener quite a lot about the underlying structure of the speech that it is accompanying. These two channels seem to be, in fact, highly integrated rather than separate.

Of course, this last experiment has its own particular limitations. It did not try to assess the power of iconic gestures generated from different viewpoints when they are presented alongside speech, but only when they are presented in isolation from speech. So the next experiment to be carried out really suggested itself. At the same time we tried to answer the question of why we use observer viewpoint gestures at all, given that they don't appear anything like as effective as character viewpoint gestures for communication purposes, with possibly one or two exceptions that really stood out.

The same 30 iconic gestures were used as in the previous experiment and were either shown in combination with the speech that they accompanied or the speech extracts were played on their own. Again great care was taken in the scoring of the responses of the participants. Below is an example of how a participant's answer was scored. This example was taken from the video condition (where the gesture–speech combination was played to the participant).

she starts [spewing bubbles]
Iconic: fingers on both hands point towards mouth area then point upwards away from mouth.

After viewing the above gesture in the video condition one participant wrote 'Somebody begins to spew bubbles out of their mouth and the bubbles move upwards away from their mouth.' Here the gesture was scored as having conveyed information to this participant about the categories *identity* (bubbles), *description of action* (spewing), *shape* (round), *movement* (yes), *direction* (upwards), and *relative position* (moving away from the mouth). No information was provided by the participant about the *speed* at which the bubbles were moving or about the *size* of the bubbles.

This experiment found that the overall mean accuracy score in the video condition, where participants could see the iconic gestures in addition to hearing the speech, was 56.8 per cent, whereas in the speech-only condition it was 48.6 per cent. Therefore again there was a significant increase in information obtained about the semantic properties of the original cartoon when the iconic gestures are added to the speech. The overall percentage increase from the speech-only condition to the video condition for character viewpoint gestures was 10.6 per cent, but it was only half that – 5.7 per cent – for observer viewpoint gestures. Statistical tests revealed that character viewpoint gestures and observer viewpoint gestures both added a significant amount of information to speech, but character viewpoint gestures added more.

When the analysis was deconstructed to individual semantic categories, it was found that *relative position*, *size*, *identity*, *movement*, *direction* and *description of action* were communicated more effectively by character viewpoint gestures than by observer viewpoint gestures, whereas *shape* and *speed* were communicated more effectively by observer viewpoint gestures than by character viewpoint gestures.

This experiment again demonstrated that iconic gestures contain significant amounts of information. One aspect of iconic gestures that does influence their communicative effectiveness was also identified. It was found in the previous experiment that when iconic gestures were shown without their accompanying speech, character viewpoint gestures were significantly more communicative than observer viewpoint gestures, but here it was also found that character viewpoint gestures were more communicative when they were displayed alongside speech. Character viewpoint gestures were particularly good again at conveying information about the semantic category *relative position*. Verbal clauses associated with character viewpoint gestures seem to be particularly poor at conveying relative position information, but the accompanying gestures more than make up for this.

The present study found that things like *size*, *identity*, *movement*, *direction* and *description of action* were communicated more effectively by character viewpoint gestures than by observer viewpoint gestures. However, despite the overall communicational advantage of character viewpoint gestures, observer viewpoint gestures were actually better at communicating additional information about *speed* and *shape*. This might be because observer viewpoint gestures can show speed relative to a stationary observer and observer viewpoint gestures enable the shape of something to be mapped out with the hands – as if an observer was directly looking at something. The categories speed and shape did not reach overall statistical significance however due to the fact that, although some observer viewpoint gestures were very effective at communicating information about these categories, this effectiveness was not consistent across all observer viewpoint gestures.

One of the most interesting findings of this study was that there was no significant correlation, across gestures, between the increase in the percentage of correct answers in going from the speech-only condition to the video condition and the amount of accurate information transmitted in the gesture-only condition. The fact that there were no significant correlations here suggests that there is an important interaction between speech and gesture in the communication of meaning, rather than a fixed amount of information contained in the iconic gesture. In other words, speech and gesture clearly interact in complex ways in the communication of meaning.

A more detailed analysis of the data reveals that there are some gestures which are highly communicative in the absence of speech, but once speech is added their contribution to the communication of meaning becomes almost redundant. In addition, there are gestures that do not communicate in the absence of speech but do communicate effectively once the speech has signalled the current theme that is being articulated. There are also some gestures that are consistently effective in terms of communication in both situations, and others that are consistently ineffective in both.

Let me try to give you some idea of the number of gestures falling into each of these four categories. In order to do this, I rank ordered the communicative effectiveness of each gesture on their own and in terms of what they added to speech. I found that five gestures were good communicators in the gesture-only condition but poor communicators when they were added to speech; three of these gestures were produced from an observer viewpoint. There were also five gestures that were poor communicators in the gesture-only condition but good communicators when they were added to speech (again three of these were produced from an observer viewpoint). There were ten gestures that were good communicators in both conditions and seven of these were produced from a character viewpoint. In the final cell there were ten gestures that were poor communicators in both conditions, six of these were produced from an observer viewpoint.

An example of the category containing gestures that work better in the gesture-only condition than they do when they are added to speech is:

bouncing the ball [on the ground]
Iconic: palm of right hand points downwards; hand moves rapidly downwards and upwards three times.

When this character viewpoint gesture was shown in the gesture-only condition it was found to convey a good deal of information about six semantic categories (namely, *identity* 'a ball'; *description of action* 'bouncing'; *shape* 'round'; *movement* 'yes'; *direction* 'up and down'; *relative position* 'the ball moving up and down between the hand and the ground'). Once speech was added to the gesture, however, the gesture became redundant with respect to all six of these semantic categories (although interestingly *speed*, i.e. the fact that the ball was being bounced very quickly, only tended to be mentioned in the video rather than in the gesture-only condition). In neither the gesture-only nor the video condition did participants get the *size* of the object correct; it was, in fact, a large ball. The overall percentage accuracy score for this gesture was 50.5 per cent in the gesture-only condition, whereas it was 75.0 per cent in the speech-only condition, increasing to 82.5 per cent in the video condition. The gesture therefore only added 7.5 per cent additional information to the speech.

Below is an example of an observer viewpoint gesture that was good at communicating information about *shape* (44 per cent accuracy) in gesture-only condition, but once the speech was added the gesture becomes redundant (zero per cent additional information about *shape* and only 2.5 per cent overall additional information).

it's got two [long bench either side]
Iconic: hands are close together, palms are pointing towards each other, hands move apart in a horizontal direction.

In gesture only this communicated to participants that the object being described was long (with very little information about what the object actually was), but when the speech was added the information provided by the gesture was clearly redundant.

On the other hand, some gestures can only successfully communicate about certain semantic categories once the speech has first provided some basic information. Below is an example of an observer viewpoint gesture that was relatively poor at communicating information about *speed*, or any of the other semantic categories, in gesture only. However, once the speech was added, the gesture then became more than just a flick of the hand – it became a male running very quickly out of his house, thus demonstrating the importance of the global meaning of the gesture in determining the meaning of the individual components of the gesture.

[runs out of his house] again
Iconic: thumb of right hand is pointing upwards, other fingers are curled together. Hand moves upwards slightly and then to the right in a rapid movement.

In the gesture-only condition 14 per cent of the participants correctly identified the *speed* of this action, whereas in the video condition 90 per cent got this right (with zero per cent in the speech-only condition).

There are also a number of cases where the gesture conveyed a good deal of information both in isolation from speech and working alongside speech. For example:

[and gets covered in soup]
Iconic: hands move to a position in front of the face; they then move apart and follow the curve of the face.

When this gesture was added to its accompanying speech, it provided participants with information about the *relative position* of the soup with respect to the character. It is the character's face that gets covered in soup. The gesture also demonstrated the *direction* in which the soup was moving and the *size* of the area that gets covered in soup. In the gesture-only condition the gesture conveyed information to participants about the same semantic categories, even though in this case they do not know what it is that is actually covering the face.

So this gesture not only conveyed important information both in isolation and alongside speech, but also conveyed information about the same semantic categories in both cases. However, there are other gestures that are very effective at communicating when they are presented both with speech and in isolation from speech, but they convey information about quite different semantic categories in the two different cases. This relationship is exemplified by the following character viewpoint gesture:

by [pulling on his tie]
Iconic: left hand moves quickly upwards; hand closes and a sharp downwards movement is made.

This gesture provided participants with information over and above that conveyed by the speech, particularly about the *speed* of the action (fast) and the *relative position* of the physical entities (the hand being wrapped around the tie). In the gesture-only condition, however, the gesture provided participants with information that mainly concerned

the *size* of the object involved (small) and the *shape* of the
object involved (long).

Some gestures are relatively poor at communicating
information in isolation from speech and are still poor when
they are added to speech. The observer viewpoint gesture
below is an extreme example of this.

the [roof starts cracking]
*Iconic: index finger of left hand points vertically upwards, other
fingers and thumb are slightly curled. Index finger moves to his
left and then to his right.*

It seems that when this type of gesture is presented without
speech the gesture is simply too abstract for a participant to
glean much information from it. Once the speech is added,
it is clear to participants what the gesture is referring to, but
now the gesture does not add any additional information to
that already contained in the speech.

In summary these experiments have found that iconic
gestures do indeed have a significant communicative function. Although both character viewpoint gestures and
observer viewpoint gestures are communicative, character
viewpoint gestures have a communicational advantage over
observer viewpoint gestures, particularly about relative
position. It was found that the speech associated with character viewpoint gestures is particularly poor at conveying
relative position information, but that the character viewpoint
gesture more than adequately makes up for this and enables
relative position information to be communicated very successfully to participants. It was also observed that there
were no significant correlations between the amount of
information that gestures add to speech and the amount of
information they convey in the absence of speech, which
suggests that there are a number of quite different relationships between the linguistic and gestural codes. In some
cases the communicative effectiveness of the gesture
depends wholly on the presence of the speech; in other
cases the speech is much less necessary. The relationship
between gestural viewpoint and the communication of

individual semantic features was discovered to be a good deal more complex than a number of psychologists had anticipated. The strength of these experiments is that it is now more precisely known what semantic information is actually received by decoders from speech and from gesture and hence it is felt that the current analyses provide a much better insight into how the linguistic and gestural codes interact in the communication of meaning.

The implications of this set of experiments are, however, quite clear. Gestures are a window on the human mind because there is now detailed experimental evidence that there is a great deal of important information in these iconic gestures, which is never articulated in speech itself. As McNeill (2000: 139) states: 'Utterances possess two sides, only one of which is speech; the other is imagery, actional and visuo-spatial. To exclude the gesture side, as has been traditional, is tantamount to ignoring half of the message out of the brain.'

This research has also demonstrated that some people seem to miss out on this information in the gesture channel almost completely; others are tuned in to it and quite unconsciously process this important information along with the speech itself. The differences in terms of the amount of information received between those who use the gestural information and those who do not is quite staggering.

In the next chapter, we will quite consciously and deliberately consider all of the messages out of the brain and not just the speech itself. In order to do this we will return to the tapes of the *Big Brother* series in which the contestants revealed a good deal more than they thought on many, many occasions. We will also consider Bill Clinton when he was President of the USA, a man whose actions often revealed much more than he and his speech ever intended.

A glimpse of the unguarded mind in action *10*

In this chapter I will put some iconic gestures of famous people, including the *Big Brother* contestants, under the microscope to see what their gestures add to the communication and in particular to see what they really reveal about their unarticulated thinking. This is a reading of fast, fleeting, dynamic body language, closely integrated with speech, sometimes gone in a fraction of a second, but full of meaning and significance.

Let us start with Bill Clinton, when he was still President of the United States. In this first example, he is in Germany meeting a whole series of German dignitaries. The occasion is very formal. Each dignitary in turn introduces himself to Clinton. 'Good morning, President Clinton, I am the German Chief of Defence Staff.' Helmut Kohl, who was then the German Chancellor, is waiting his turn patiently. The two men obviously know each other; this will be a somewhat more relaxed introduction in an otherwise formal gathering. The German Chancellor steps forward. 'I'm the German Chancellor,' he says, with a smile, offering his hand. Clinton shakes his hand and the two men grasp each other's arms in a sign of friendship, while he says, 'I was thinking of you last night, Helmut, because I watched the sumo wrestling on television.'

This is translated for Chancellor Kohl, who responds by stepping back. His facial expression shows that he is not particularly pleased with the comment. His smile fades rapidly. But what Clinton has said so far is not entirely unambiguous. He may have thought of Herr Kohl when he was watching the sumo wrestling for a number of quite different, and as yet unspecified, reasons. Perhaps it was the first moment he had to relax all that day; perhaps it was just his first opportunity to think of anybody in his hectic schedule. Surely, it wasn't because Herr Kohl was large like a sumo wrestler; surely it wasn't this essential similarity that reminded Clinton of the German Chancellor. Bill Clinton's next utterance, and in particular the iconic gesture that accompanies the speech, tells us and unfortunately Chancellor Kohl, who happened to notice the gesture, exactly what Clinton had in mind.

BILL CLINTON: <u>you and I [are the biggest people here]</u>

Iconic: fingers, on both hands, are together and slightly curled up; both hands move away from the front of the body and then away from each other; fingers start to spread apart, and a very large circle is formed.

Any ambiguity in being 'the biggest people here' is resolved by the iconic gesture, which indicates that the aspect of size that Clinton had in mind here was girth. The iconic gesture in fact depicted a huge girth. It might not be too embarrassing to be described as 'big', as in big and powerful like a sumo wrestler, which is all that Clinton's speech actually says. It is only the iconic gesture that reveals that what Clinton was really thinking was that Chancellor Kohl is extremely large in the girth like a sumo wrestler. The Chancellor's facial expression after he notices the gesture shows that he is really very displeased. He fails to mask this displeasure with any kind of false smile. Clinton seems to realize that he has revealed a good deal more than he intended here and continues his lonely greeting of the German dignitaries with a look of some embarrassment on his face.

Let's now move away from Bill Clinton and back inside the *Big Brother* house to consider some incidents from the very first week in the house from the second series. The first couple of weeks are a critical time in the *Big Brother* house because the housemates want to make as favourable an impression as possible on each other and on the viewers. As part of my analyses for the programme I had studied how each of the housemates used false smiles to create a good impression and to cover up their real emotion. The housemates were also all very carefully monitoring what they said during these critical days in the house. Many of the segments of speech were, however, accompanied by iconic gestures, which revealed much more about the housemates' thinking than they probably realized. Sometimes we just get additional information by studying the gesture and nothing too revealing or embarrassing, but sometimes we get a lot more than this.

In the example below from *Big Brother 2*, Penny is in the kitchen with Dean, Bubble and Brian during the first week in the house. The housemates are discussing the fact that Penny has cooked every meal so far. It is, in fact, something of a criticism because Penny is perceived as having attempted to take control in the house by making herself indispensable through her willingness to cook.

PENNY: [Can we all sit down] and delegate a meal
Iconic: index finger on right hand extended slightly, other fingers are more curled up. Hand moves in a large, anti-clockwise arc in front of the chest.

This is an attempt to deflect criticism by saying that who does the cooking should be democratically elected by the group. In terms of her language, the focus is very much on democracy and consensus, but her gesture tells a different story. Penny, in fact, uses a character viewpoint gesture to show how the group should arrange itself, i.e. in a large arc around her, with herself as the natural focus of her regard. The gesture indicates her preferred *relative position* of the housemates with regard to her. This can be compared with what Stuart actually did in the first week in the house in the second series when he arranged the group in a similar sort of arc around himself to discuss how much to bet on the fire task. This particular spatial arrangement had put Stuart firmly in control of the group. Penny wants to be in control in the same kind of way; her gesture tells us that. She says that she wants democracy to reign, but it is democracy on her terms, with the group all arranged around her and looking directly at her, so that she can control them with her eye gaze. The iconic gesture here probably revealed more about her thinking and her intentions at this point than she realized.

Also during the first week in the house in *Big Brother 2*, Amma and Stuart are in the kitchen discussing the shopping list. Amma is explaining that all of the housemates should make more of a contribution to the list, rather than letting one person take sole responsibility for it. Penny had taken charge of the first shopping list.

> AMMA: <u>Next time we need to read out the list and say</u>
> <u>'Do we want it? No.' 'Do we want it? Yes.'</u>
> <u>as opposed to [one person going down the list]</u>

Iconic: index and middle fingers on left hand extended slightly, other fingers curled up. Hand moves rapidly downwards from above head to chest level.

<u>and saying 'How about some of that?'</u>

Here, Amma's character viewpoint gesture reveals the *speed* at which Penny went through the list; the gesture depicts the very rapid speed of this process. This is what Amma is criticizing here; her view that the other housemates are not being given the opportunity to change or affect what is on the list. She doesn't mention in her speech that Penny went through the shopping list too quickly; it is her iconic gesture here that reveals her private thoughts on this matter.

In a further incident in the first week in the house in the second series, Paul, Stuart, Bubble and Brian are in the garden attending the fire that has to be kept lit for five days – this was the housemates' first task. They are discussing the fact that Brian and Paul have just used the handle of the axe as firewood, which might not seem the most sensible course of action. Paul attempts to defend that decision, accompanying his defence with an iconic gesture.

> PAUL: <u>we used the [handle of the axe as extra wood] in case we ran out.</u>

Iconic: fingers on the right hand are slightly curled and palm is facing upwards; hand moves up and down five times in front of body.

This is a slightly unfortunate character viewpoint gesture from Paul, because it reminds everyone of what the wooden handle of an axe really is – the gesture depicts somebody holding an axe by its handle. It primarily conveys information about the *relative position* of the hand and the handle. After all the wooden handle of an axe is both the handle of an important implement in a house, especially in a house where the task is to keep a fire going at all times, and *at the same time* it is also a piece of wood that will burn like any other piece of wood. There are two ways that we can think of a wooden handle in the context of having to keep a fire going. In his speech, Paul defends the action of himself and Brian by saying that the handle was just 'extra wood'. His iconic gesture reveals, however, that he really thought primarily of the handle not as 'extra wood' but as one bit of the axe that is crucial to making it work. A different sort of iconic gesture would have been necessary to tell us that Paul thought of the handle primarily as extra wood.

One of the most memorable moments during the housemates' first week in the second series occurred in the garden when Stuart, Narinder, Helen and Elizabeth were discussing their most embarrassing moments. This was an opportunity for each of the housemates to tell the other housemates about themselves – the kinds of things that they got up to before entering the house, the kinds of lives that they had led previously, really the kind of person that they were. Elizabeth asks Stuart about his most embarrassing moment. Stuart's account is full of highly revealing iconic gestures.

ELIZABETH: What was your most embarrassing moment then?

STUART: Well, we had a works do and I got a bit amorous and sort of got into the lift. We thought we'd stop the lift halfway.

ELIZABETH: Is this with your wife?

STUART: Yeah. We thought we'd stop this lift halfway between floors.

NARINDER: Why?

STUART: Because this is my most embarrassing moment.

NARINDER: To have sex?

STUART: [In this hotel]

Preparation phase: right hand rises upwards with palm facing downwards and fingers straight. Hand stops at shoulder level.

STUART: And we didn't realize it but the lift very slowly just descended.

HELEN: And were you doing it in the lift?

STUART: [Nods]. And suddenly I'm conscious that the doors are opening.

NARINDER: And you're having sex? You're joking.

STUART: And there's a crowd of people and I thought 'oh no'. And I'm [desperately trying to hit the button. And I just turned round and said 'We are married you know'.]

Iconic: thumb of right hand pointing slightly upwards, the rest of the fingers on this hand are curled and tightly together. Hand is at waist level and stabs sharply and frantically away from body eight times.

STUART: And when we came down for breakfast in the morning – looking round [. . . pause . . .] we'd got our shades on, and going 'oh please'.

Iconic: both hands are curled up to form fists. Hands rise to position next to temples of head.

His first character viewpoint iconic gesture is crucial here. Stuart is ostensibly talking about his most embarrassing moment, but at the same time he is telling a set of strangers what kind of man he is. He is telling them that he is the kind of man who has sex in semi-public places. He says that he and his wife did not want to be discovered having sex in the lift, 'I'm desperately trying to hit the button', and the iconic gesture revealing his inner thoughts about the incident shows that this is exactly what he was trying to do. The gesture shows the *relative position* of the lift button and Stuart, the *speed* with which he was trying to push the button, and even the repetitious *nature of the action*. This is important here because from the other housemates' point of view Stuart may well have been a total exhibitionist in terms of sexual behaviour, who likes to have sex habitually in public view, rather than someone who just likes a little bit of excitement or danger during intimate moments. He says verbally that he was trying desperately to hit the button and his iconic gesture supports this, luckily for him.

The second iconic gesture, occurring in the pause in speech, before he explains that he went down for breakfast the next morning with his shades on to conceal his embarrassment, again supports what he is saying in his speech. This iconic gesture, depicting pulling shades up over the eyes, says that here is a man who was caught having sex and was very embarrassed as a result, rather than someone who is a complete sexual exhibitionist. Note the way that the iconic gesture corresponding to having shades on anticipates the relevant part of the verbal utterance, suggesting that this gesture was spontaneous and natural rather than an attempt to dupe his attentive audience. An analysis of the iconic gestures here tells us that Stuart was at least genuine in his account and truthful about his psychological reaction to being caught having sex. That, at least, was something. Stuart's winking behaviour displayed roughly at the same sort of time in the house was, however, something else. That was a nonverbal strategy which failed. The gestures in contrast were not merely a successful nonverbal strategy, but a glimpse into how he really remembered a particular incident in the first place, a glimpse into the real Stuart.

In the third series of *Big Brother* I got the opportunity to present some of these ideas on iconic gesture for the first time. In the first psychology show, I started with a brief introduction to how the hands can be used generally in interaction before moving on to an analysis of a particular iconic gesture. This was the first time I had commented on how revealing the hands really can be. The particular incident was a surprise eviction that had been foisted onto the housemates. The catch, and with *Big Brother* there usually is a catch, is that the housemates themselves had to decide who was to be evicted. I analysed the role of the hands in this process.

Show of hands

The announcement of the surprise eviction has deeply shaken the *Big Brother* housemates. This was completely unanticipated and has produced a strong response in them. And we see, perhaps for the first time, real spontaneous emotions and their unplanned thinking in action. The hands are a crucial part of body language and it is during this critical time that the hands come into play. They are used for control, communication and concealment.

Control

The group have to decide on the procedure they're going to use to make their decision. Getting your voice heard is crucial and the hands provide a powerful device for obtaining and holding the floor. When they were asked to make their decision they literally hold onto each other for support and comfort but once they realize they have a decision to make everyone frees their hands – they need their hands at work.

Communication

Hands and arms have other functions – they articulate thoughts that never actually appear in the speech itself. These are called iconic gestures. This can be seen with Spencer when he grabs control of the debate. He argues that there is no point in discussing it, they should all think about it and give one answer.

There's no point discussing it, [think about it and give one answer]

Iconic: Right hand moves upwards to area in front of chest. Palm of hand is pointing to the left. Hand moves in a clockwise direction making slight up and down movements as the hand points towards each member of the group.

FIGURE 10.1.
Spencer's hand reveals who he thinks should be the first to express their opinion.
Copyright © Channel 4.

What he doesn't say with words, he reveals with his hands. Who should talk first and what order they should talk in. His hand gesture here reveals his thinking. The voting should start with Alison and proceed round the group clockwise. Alison passes, PJ continues, followed by Adele, exactly as directed. Spencer's silent language has exerted a powerful control on the group.

Concealment

Other housemates attempt to conceal their emotions. Lee, for instance, puts on his sunglasses. Alison uses a more basic device; she hides behind her hands. Why do some housemates attempt to mask their facial expressions in this way? They might be feeling mixed emotions at this point, surprise, sadness, anxiety, perhaps tinged with elation, after all it's not them up for eviction at this point. The unexpected eviction has been very revealing, despite the attempts of some of the housemates to conceal how they feel. But the hands will always give the game away.

This was my first attempt to suggest that an analysis of the iconic gestures that accompany speech can be quite revealing. My next analysis, I thought, was a good deal more interesting. This was the famous, or infamous, morning after the night before when Jade had performed oral sex on PJ (in the piece I did not admit that I knew exactly what had occurred). They had both been drinking fairly large quantities of alcohol. This really was the office party scenario. The *Big Brother* cameras caught them waking up and starting to come to terms with what had occurred the night before.

A night to remember

We don't know exactly what happened between Jade and PJ in the poor bedroom earlier this week, but what's undeniable is that something happened. PJ finally gave in to Jade's attentions and the outcome is a typical office party scenario. This is the morning after when two people are trying to come to terms with what's happened.

It's not just what PJ says that tells us something about his thoughts and feelings. PJ's iconic hand gestures also tell us something about his real feelings for Jade and what passed between them. He says, 'What happened was I went like this and I kissed you.

What happened was [I went like this and I kissed you]
Iconic: At head level hands and arms move away from each other, until they are wide apart. Fingers are spread open with palms are pointing towards each other.

The right hand represents PJ, the left hand represents Jade; the distance between the hands tell us something about his view of the real level of intimacy. The hands representing PJ and Jade never come together. PJ is acting like the typical man after the office party. He regrets what's happened and is backing off, while boasting about the event with other people.

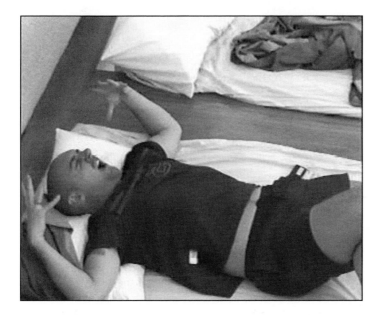

PJ: I was grabbing her and I was fucking naked, I can't believe it.

But his real feelings are a good deal more complex. In discussion with Spencer and Kate we find PJ attempting to explain why the event had occurred.

KATE: Sexual tension, had to relieve it.
PJ: Oh it wasn't relieved.

His hand gesture represents his pushing her head down (see Figure 10.3 on the following page).

I'm under the blankets with her [grabbing her head like that]
Iconic: Right hand is above head level, palm is pointing downwards. Hand moves downwards to just below chest level, then moves upwards before moving down again.

The gesture depicts PJ firmly in control of the situation, which is how he consciously wants to be seen. It is a desperate attempt to make up for the loss of control that he really feels about what happened.

On the surface Jade seems to be denying what's happened and declares that she is not willing to take this any further, but her body language reveals a different story. Jade approaches PJ in the garden. She stands right beside him to give him another opportunity to get closer to her, although he is clearly very aware of her as they both turn away at exactly the same moment. He does not respond in any positive way. She puts her arms around him but he doesn't even remove his hands from his pockets. She tries to come across as carefree by keeping one foot off the ground, but this is a rather desperate attempt to create greater intimacy between them. He rejects her intimacy unambiguously. Jade is very rejected. Being separated from Jade by the next task might be PJ's only hope to avoid further approaches and possible confrontation. Otherwise PJ is in a very vulnerable position. His brutal rejection of Jade may come back to haunt him.

The next piece revolved around interviews in the Diary Room with all four housemates who were up for eviction.

They were asked a series of standardized questions about whom they thought might be evicted that week and how they would feel if it turned out to be themselves. I focused on the behaviour of all four housemates, but it was the behaviour of Adele, who was in fact evicted, whose behaviour was probably the most interesting. Her iconic gesture, I thought, was extremely revealing here.

It's cold outside

Eviction night in the *Big Brother* house triggers a fundamental moment of reflection, as it points to one of the housemates' biggest sources of anxiety. This is the fear of the outside world, the confrontation with the big unknown that might welcome the housemates back into reality as heroes or villains.

During the day Big Brother called all four of this week's nominees to the Diary Room to face the same set of specific questions. What they say, but perhaps more importantly how they say it, reveals their true thoughts and feelings about eviction. Jade takes up a closed defensive posture throughout this succession of questions. It is only when she says she can learn from her mistakes, five minutes in, that she relaxes her posture.

As a nomination veteran Jonny takes time over his answers. His relaxed, open posture suggests that he feels comparatively safe. Kate shows a series of classic anxiety responses when confronted with her feelings if she were evicted. Whenever Kate thinks specifically about what the public might be saying about her, her posture moves from quite open to very closed right across her body. Her speech is characterized by a whole series of false starts and filled pauses. Anxiety is interfering with the formulation of her thoughts. Her thinking here reveals her competitive side and also her determination to win.

Adele says that she or Jade are the most likely to leave.

> ADELE: [So Jade, then me, then Jonny, then Kate], I think that's the order.

Iconic: Hands and arms are wide apart and resting on the arms of a chair. Left hand rises slightly with index finger pointing forwards. Right hand then rises slightly, index finger points forwards, finger moves slowly to the right and as it does so it makes three slight up and down movements.

But her unconscious iconic gesture reveals what Adele really thinks. She uses a different hand, her left, to represent Jade and her right to represent herself and the other nominees. In reality she sees a huge gap between herself and Jade. Adele has not even anticipated being evicted. When she is asked how she would feel if she were to be evicted her silent pauses and filled pauses reflect new cognitive activity. This might be the first time that she's really considered this.

What was particularly interesting about this case was that we could look for other evidence that she had not anticipated her own eviction. Evidence from her speech channel, namely the presence of silent pauses (brief periods of silence, sometimes as short as 200 milliseconds) and filled pauses ('ah', 'er', 'um', etc.), which reflect new cognitive activity (Beattie and Shovelton 2002c; Goldman-Eisler 1968) tell us that she had not previously thought about this. In other words they support the evidence from the iconic gesture.

The next example came about because of a treat offered by *Big Brother*. One housemate could receive a telephone call from their family and friends; the only problem was that the housemates had to decide amongst themselves who that person should be.

Jonny

Jonny appears to display his altruistic side most forcefully on day 51 in the group discussions about who should receive the phone call from friends and relatives.

JONNY: [We all have to pick]

Iconic: Right arm is resting along right leg. Palm of right hand is pointing upwards, fingers are close together but are stretched out. Hand moves to the right whilst making slight up and down movements; when the hand points towards Tim it stops moving and holds the position.

FIGURE 10.4.
Jonny's gesture offers Tim the chance to receive the phone call.
Copyright © Channel 4.

Jonny says 'We all have to pick' but his iconic gesture reveals that he has already decided that Tim should be the lucky one here. The gesture is an unconscious offering movement directed Tim's way. Real altruism does not involve personal gain, but Jonny does gain here by drawing attention to Tim's shortcomings, by implying that he needs a kick up the arse. He appears totally altruistic and yet he uses his altruism to denigrate Tim and to boost his own self-image simultaneously.

There are also some interesting metaphoric gestures in the *Big Brother* house, which again can reveal important aspects of the thinking of the individuals concerned. Behaviour in the Diary Room is always interesting because housemates can communicate with *Big Brother* and the millions watching at home without the other housemates' knowledge. Josh, the late arrival in the house in the second series, is in the Diary Room at the end of week three. He is explaining to *Big Brother* why he likes Elizabeth.

JOSH: [at some ends of the scale there's quite erratic people, and quite loud]

Metaphoric: fingers on both hands are extended, but not together, and point to his right. Right hand moves towards the right so that right hand is extended away from body and left hand remains in front of chest. Fingers on both hands flex backwards and forwards twice.

and she's [very calming] in her opinions.

Metaphoric: fingers on both hands are straight and quite close together. Palms are pointing towards each other and both hands move downwards in a sharp, rapid movement.

These metaphoric gestures are important because essentially they support what he is saying verbally. The metaphoric gestures, the fingers apart and flexing to represent the abstract concept of 'erratic people', and then the fingers closer together and moving straight down to represent somebody who is more straightforward and not erratic in their behaviour, distinguish types of people in essentially the same way as his speech does. The metaphoric gesture about Elizabeth adds the information that she isn't erratic but that she is straight up and down, with no sides to her. These gestures suggest that he does indeed like Elizabeth, rather than here being engaged in some secret strategy, trying to appeal to the television audience by saying that he likes Elizabeth, a woman that he might think the viewers also like. The fact that he never nominated Elizabeth for eviction would support this interpretation.

That same week, Josh is in the Diary Room explaining why he doesn't always understand Brian and Narinder's sense of humour.

> JOSH: in Brian's case it's his age and in Narinder I would
> say she's his sort of [most closely bonded person]

Metaphoric: fingers on both hands are extended; hands then move towards each other so that fingers of both hands are intertwined.

Again, this metaphoric gesture representing the relationship between Narinder and Brian supports what he is saying verbally, and reveals how closely he thinks that the two of them are intertwined in terms of their personality and behaviour. He clearly feels excluded from this relationship right at the start of his time in the *Big Brother* house, which may have had some implications for the psychological distance that grew between him and Brian during their time in the house.

Another interesting metaphoric gesture shown in the second series was displayed by Narinder in week three in the house, when she was warning Brian about Stuart, after Penny's eviction. Stuart had had an argument with Penny during the course of the first week. Stuart seems to have been perceived by some as very threatening at that time. He was after all a successful person in the outside world who appeared to be interested in taking control in the house and potentially winning the contest. The verbal context of the utterance was as follows:

BRIAN: I've seen a different side to Stuart now.
NARINDER: He's dangerous.
BRIAN: Do you think?
NARINDER: Not dangerous as in evil, but just . . .
BRIAN: Just be careful.
NARINDER: 'Cos when he started the Penny thing it was
  because he wanted Penny out . . . It's the way he does
  it.
BRIAN: Do you think?
NARINDER: [he's got his plan]

Metaphoric: index finger on left hand pointing upwards, other fingers slightly curled, hand makes a clockwise circular movement in a full circle in front of the face.

This is clearly a metaphoric gesture, the *topic* being the abstract concept, Stuart's plan, the *vehicle* being the gestural image which involves a particular space being demarcated, and the *ground* is that abstract plans can be viewed as distinct physical entities of a certain size, with boundaries, which can be either quite vague or quite definite. Stuart's plan here was depicted as medium sized, not particularly small but not all-encompassing either, and well worked out, in that the outline of the circle was sharp and clear. Narinder was revealing that she really did think of Stuart as a dangerous man with clear plans in his head and it is interesting that she nominated him for eviction at the end of that week. The gesture again holds a clue as to her thinking here; it offers a glimpse into her paranoia.

Another perhaps more obvious metaphoric gesture was displayed by Elizabeth in week four in the *Big Brother* house. She was talking about the new arrival Josh to Brian, Amma and Helen in the girls' bedroom. She used the following gesture–speech combination. Brian's reply is also included:

[he's very outgoing]
Metaphoric: fingers on both hands are slightly curved and wide open. Both hands touch respective shoulders, then both rapidly move away from body.

[he's very confident]
Metaphoric: fingers on both hands are still slightly curved and open and hands move away from the front of the body.

BRIAN: I think he's lovely.

In this case, the *topic*, the abstract concept being discussed, was Josh's personality; the *vehicle* being the space demarcated from the body; the *ground* is that certain types of personality – extravert or outgoing versus introvert – can be viewed as taking up more or less space in everyday interaction. 'Outgoing' as a description of personality is shown metaphorically to be taking up more space going out from the person. Her metaphoric gestures support what she is saying verbally about Josh rather than being just an attempt to influence the other housemates with her comments.

Dean, on the other hand, displays a significant number of beats in the Diary Room, during week seven in the second series, when he is describing how difficult he will find the following day's nominations.

DEAN: There's two people I would never nominate left in the house. So in that way the choice is kind of made up for me, but it's [not easy now, it's really, really not easy].

Beat: fingers on left hand are curled up and close together. Hand makes eight slight up and down movements by the left-hand side of the stomach.

Beats do, of course, seem like the simplest form of gesture that people ever display, but nevertheless they can be highly revealing. The simplicity of their form, as I have argued earlier, belies their real importance. They accompany the most significant parts of the speech from the speaker's point of view. Thus, even beats with their regular and simple form may provide some clue as to the inner workings of the mind of the speaker. The presence of beats in this part of Dean's speech would suggest that he really does believe that the nomination process at this point in the proceedings is not that easy any longer. He could of course by making this statement just be making a plea to the television audience that deep down inside he really is a nice guy who doesn't actually enjoy the nomination process. But the presence of the beats at certain points in his speech would indicate that this second hypothesis is probably not correct.

In *Celebrity Big Brother 2*, broadcast in November 2002, a number of British celebrities went into the *Big Brother* house for a period of ten days for charity. The eventual winner was Mark Owen, former member of boy band Take That. This show provided some extraordinary examples of iconic gestures for analysis.

One of the most striking features of this particular show was the behaviour of the comedian and game show host, Les Dennis. Here we will analyse some of Les Dennis's iconic and metaphoric gestures to get a glimpse of how he thinks about his life and his relationships both inside and outside the *Big Brother* house, as well as the behaviour of some of his fellow housemates.

Here is some of the action, and a little of the preceding context. Readers might like to attempt to interpret some of the gestures for themselves at this point in the book.

Les is in the Diary Room and because he gained a score of zero in a quiz set by *Big Brother* he is the only housemate who has to do the nominating for the forthcoming eviction. He is explaining why this nomination process is so difficult for him.

LES: We [are all six of us, very, very, close]
Metaphoric: Left hand is in front of left shoulder, palm is pointing forwards and fingers are straight and apart. Hand moves quickly to the left away from the body and then moves quickly back to its position in front of shoulder. This whole movement is repeated twice. The first half of the movement is then produced for a third time and the hand now remains away from the body.

[really close]
Metaphoric: Hands are wide apart, palms point towards each other. Hands move rapidly towards each other to an area in front of stomach but hands don't touch – they stop when they are about six inches apart.

I analysed Les's gestures on *Celebrity Big Brother* and I made the following point: 'Well the problem with this is he's saying that the housemates are all very, very close, so you would expect the gesture to be towards the body but the first gesture is actually away from the body. Then when he says "really close" the distance between his hands tells us how close the housemates are – which is not close at all. If the housemates had been close the hands should have drawn together.'

Here is another example. Anne Diamond, a former presenter of the *Good Morning* television programme, is standing in the *Big Brother* kitchen drinking coffee in her blue towelling dressing-gown. Les Dennis appears from the boys' bedroom looking sleepy and carrying a soap bag and a towel. Les greets Anne with a hug and starts to talk about how bad he is feeling about having nominated her and Sue for eviction after getting a score of nought in a quiz set by *Big Brother*.

LES: [Something's just occurred to me]
Metaphoric: the right hand is just above shoulder level with the index finger extended, the other fingers and the thumb are clenched. The index finger is pointing and the hand is moving quickly backwards and forwards.

[though]
Self-adaptor: the index finger of the right hand is pressed against the lips; the other fingers and the thumb are clenched.

[the fault with that]
Metaphoric: the right hand is just above shoulder level. The index finger and thumb are extended and are about three inches apart as

if grasping an imaginary object. The hand moves down in steps until the hand is at chest level.

[doing that is]
Metaphoric: index finger is in front of the chest, finger moves about three inches towards the left and then moves three inches downwards.

[I could have thrown it]
Metaphoric: the index finger and thumb are still extended and make an arch-like movement upwards towards the left.

ANNE: In what way?

LES: [to stay in]
Metaphoric: the index finger of the right hand is extended and makes an arch-like movement downwards and to the right-hand side.

by getting three [by getting nought]
Metaphoric: the thumb is extended away from the fingers of the right hand; the hand makes a sweeping movement away from the body and to the right-hand side.

[It could be a devious plot]
Metaphoric: the fingers and thumb of the right hand are clenched together and move up and down.

ANNE: It ensures that you stay in but the price you pay is that you have to nominate two others.

LES: [I didn't throw it, I didn't throw it, don't, you wouldn't ever think I threw it would] you?
Self-adaptor: the right hand moves up to the head and scratches the head.

This is an important conversation for Les. He wishes to repair any negative perceptions that Anne Diamond might have of him because of his performance in the task set by Big Brother; a task that he might have deliberately failed to safeguard his position in the house.

There are a number of iconic and metaphoric gestures and some self-adaptors, or self-touching movements, accompanying his speech. I will just comment on some of the more striking ones. The first metaphoric gesture is interesting because he says 'something's just occurred to me', and the metaphoric gesture does display the rapid *speed* of this process. This might be interpreted as indicating that his thoughts on this matter were very recent and that he hadn't been thinking about the consequences of failing the task *before* he'd taken it. If Les had thought about these consequences earlier he could be accused of deliberately failing the task so that he could stay in the *Big Brother* house for longer. This metaphoric gesture works because the *topic*, the abstract concept of thought occurring in one's head, is portrayed using the *vehicle* of a particular gestural image which critically involves movement, with the *ground* being that thoughts have different speeds and trajectories in the gestural space.

Then he says 'the fault with that', where the position of the fingers in the gestural space represent his understanding of the size or the nature of the fault. The fingers are approximately three inches apart, which in his mind seems to suggest that such a fault would not be insignificant.

Another metaphoric gesture accompanying 'It could be a devious plot' is constituted by a clenched fist. The *topic* of the metaphoric gesture is the nature of the plot, the *vehicle* being the gestural image which involves a certain positioning of the fingers; the *ground* here for this metaphoric gesture is that plots can be more or less open or closed – 'devious plots' like this one are tight and closed like a fist.

Did Les Dennis, in fact, deliberately fail in the task? It is difficult to say, but what is clear is that he recognizes that other housemates' perceptions here are very significant and that it could potentially be quite difficult for him in the *Big Brother* house if the other housemates thought that he had thrown it.

Here is a different example. The comedian Sue Perkins has just gone back to bed in the girls' bedroom after becoming annoyed during Les Dennis's impression of former Take That member, Mark Owen, in the kitchen area. She is lying in bed when Melinda Messenger walks in and checks to see how Sue is feeling. Sue sits up and expresses annoyance at Les's behaviour.

> SUE: I think I just very [fractionally got tired of the sound of his voice for a second]

Metaphoric: the thumb and the index finger of the right hand join together to form an O shape; the other fingers are extended. The hand moves down and the thumb and index finger move apart. The hand then moves back up to around head height and the index finger and thumb come together again to form the O shape.

and just sort of just thought [please stop performing]
Iconic: the right arm is extended out with the palm facing away from the body. The fingers are slightly spread.

[Enough]
Metaphoric: the right hand moves into the body and then extends out with more forceful repetition of gesture.

[Shh]
Iconic: the index finger of the right hand is pressed against the lips.

This series of gestures, which are all closely connected, display the strength of Sue's feelings about wanting Les to stop 'performing'. The iconic and metaphoric gestures show the forcefulness of her desire. The end point of the metaphoric gesture in the gestural space, with the arm fully extended, could be interpreted as indicating that Sue wishes to maintain some distance from Les's behaviour (quite literally at arm's length).

Melinda Messenger, Anne Diamond and Les Dennis are sitting in the living room area of the *Big Brother* house. Melinda is doing her make-up, while Anne sits in her dressing-gown. Melinda begins by talking about the day she was contacted by *The Sun* newspaper to be a page three model. The conversation moves on to the way in which individuals are 'pigeon-holed' by the British media. Les thinks that this is particularly true of his wife, Amanda Holden. He begins to talk about public perceptions of her following her much talked about affair with Neil Morrissey.

LES: I feel it more for Amanda, you know, because I think that she has had a bad rap as far as, you know, [I've said it before]

Beat: the index finger of the right hand is extended and pointing, the other fingers and thumb are clenched. The hand moves up and down.

[it was one incident],
Iconic: index finger still extended moves up and down.

it was a short time and then since then she's made to be this bad girl [that she is not, do you know what I mean and that is the hardest thing]
Beat: gesture is repeated with more force.

it's not, you know, what comes with you, where you started in your job and what it is professionally, it's what comes along that [they try to]
Iconic: fingers on right hand are slightly curved and apart, palm is pointing downwards; hand and arm move downwards.

[they try to forge an image for you]
Metaphoric: the index finger and the thumb of the right hand are extended, but the tip of the index finger is bent towards the thumb. The finger and the thumb are about two inches apart as if holding an imaginary object. The hand moves up and down.

that every time [people meet her]
Metaphoric: the index finger and thumb are still extended they come together and then move way from each other until they are approximately three inches apart.

[she has to] prove that she isn't that
Metaphoric: the right hand is extended with the palm of the hand
facing upwards. The hand moves down.

[I just get so] frustrated
Metaphoric: the fingers of both hands are extended and apart, both
hands move up and over to the left hand side. The upper body
turns to follow the movement of the hands.

This particular set of iconic and metaphoric gestures are fascinating because they provide a wonderful window into how Les Dennis thinks about the media in terms of their treatment of his wife Amanda Holden. When Les says 'they try to' his gesture appears to represent a claw – his hand moves downwards and his fingers are curved and apart, he views the media as 'preying' on his wife, his wife as victim. The metaphoric gesture accompanying 'they try to form an image for you' shows the nature of the image. The positioning of the fingers in the gestural space, approximately two inches apart with the tip of the index finger bent over, shows exactly how restricted the image actually is, in Les's mind.

Les Dennis and Sue Perkins are swinging on the bench in the *Big Brother* garden. They are talking about Sue's time at university and Les mentions that he feels he needs to do a course to help build his confidence for writing.

> LES: Well I'd love to get into, 'cause I'm frightened of writing. I wouldn't mind creative writing or something like that.
> SUE: You should definitely do that. Why are you frightened of writing?
> LES: Dunno.
> SUE: Are you frightened of speaking?
> LES: Er, no, it's just sitting in front of, I do write occasionally and when I do write I'm really tough on myself, if I draw [I go ahh that's shit and I throw it away]

Iconic: the hands are spread apart with the fingers spread and the
palms of each are facing each other. The hands come together and

the motion mimics someone screwing up a piece of paper. The left hand extends out to the left as if throwing the paper away.

[you know]
Self-adaptor: the left hand moves to the head and the hand scratches the head.

[and if I write something]
Iconic: the left hand is still scratching the head. The right hand is at shoulder level with the fingers extended and spread. The palm faces the left.

[I go nah that's rubbish and I throw it away]
Iconic: the left hand moves to the right-hand side over the right hand that moves to the left-hand side. The left hand then moves down until it is almost touching the right hand and extends out as if throwing something to the left.

These character viewpoint iconic gestures portray the physical act of throwing away the work with some vigour. It tells us that he is not just merely saying that he rejects his own work in any non-literal or metaphorical sense; rather that he physically discards it with some force. The force of the movement gives us some idea of how he views the quality of his own work and tells us a great deal about what kind of a self-critical person Les really is.

Reading iconic gestures is a fascinating and hitherto unconscious human cognitive activity. But there is one important question that I have not raised yet, which is the issue of whether iconic gestures and beats can be faked to mislead and dupe others. I would argue that it is really quite difficult to fake iconic gestures when you are lying. It is very complicated to split meaning into the verbal and gestural channels in a way that might look natural or normal and get the division of meaning between the two channels just right, as well as the precise iconic form of the gesture and the right degree of anticipation of the associated part of the verbal message by the preparation phase of the gesture. Research in psychology on the nonverbal behaviours associated with lying is sometimes a little bit disappointing because those researchers who work on lying tend not to carry out the very detailed kinds of analyses of language and gesture that we are considering here. Rather, they often simply count the frequency of gestures, often not even properly distinguishing between the different types of gesture. Research in this area suggests that generally speaking gesture frequency decreases when people are lying (Cody and O'Hair 1983; Davis and Hadiks 1995; Ekman 1988; Ekman and Friesen 1972; Ekman, Friesen and Scherer 1976; Ekman, O'Sullivan, Friesen and Scherer 1991; Greene, O'Hair, Cody and Yen 1985; Hofer, Kohnken, Hanewinkel and Bruhn 1993; Kalma, Witte and Zaalberg 1996; Mann, Vrij and Bull 1998; Vrij, Edward, Roberts and Bull 1999; but see Bond, Kahler and Paolicelli 1985; deTurck and Miller 1985), suggesting perhaps that liars do not want to risk giving the game away through revealing hand movements. Therefore they try to inhibit this form of behaviour by clasping their hands or using similar kinds of strategy. Aldert Vrij (2000) has a useful summary of this research in his book *Detecting Lies and Deceit*. He also summarizes the empirical evidence that most people believe that gesture frequency actually increases during deception, which shows that most people have a false belief here. My guess is that if the hands are not prevented from gesturing in this way, then the precise form of the iconic gesture, which has never been considered in any great detail in the research on deception, could potentially be highly revealing when people are lying. I have a number of specific anecdotes here to support this. Anecdotes are never the best basis for a psychological theory, but sometimes they can be quite useful nonetheless. The first example comes from a meeting at a public relations company that I attended where one of the executives was talking about the sales of a particular product after their campaign had finished. She said:

the sales after that campaign [started to soar]
Iconic: right hand makes upward trajectory but falls fractionally at the top most part of the trajectory. The slight fall depicted in the gesture corresponding to the word 'soar'.

The iconic gesture seemed to contradict what she was saying in her speech. I actually interrupted the meeting at this point to query whether sales had indeed soared as she had said or had declined, as I guessed. She hesitated, slightly embarrassed, and admitted that I was in fact correct. Sales had declined immediately after the campaign, 'but they picked up again' she added defensively. I was praised, if that's the right word, for my perceptiveness.

Here is another anecdotal example. A female friend was telling me about her experiences at a party where a close friend's boyfriend had kissed her. Here is what she said:

and he [kissed me] on the cheek
Iconic: fingers of right hand outstretched and close together, thumb curled in towards palm. Hand moves towards mouth and fingertips touch right-hand side of lips.

Since the person who kissed her was the boyfriend of a very close friend, she seemingly did not want to admit that this kiss was in any way intimate. The speech was under strict editorial control; she said exactly what she intended to. The iconic gesture was under much less strict editorial control and indicated the *relative position* of both sets of lips. This was not a kiss on the cheek, no matter what she said. I queried this and she looked astonished to be challenged in this way. 'You weren't there,' she said. 'How do you know?' I pointed out her gesture to her and she said that she didn't even realize that she had made a gesture in the first place.

This hypothesis that the precise form of iconic gestures may have a role to play in the detection of deception has formed the basis of a recent experiment. In this experiment, participants were shown a number of cartoons with par-ticular events depicted in them. They had to narrate the story as before. Then they had to narrate the story, which was still projected onto a screen in front of them, for a second time. This time they had to change some of the critical details and attempt to persuade another person that these changed details were actually part of the real story. For example, in one picture a boy was dribbling a football around an opponent in a circle. In the second telling the narrator had to recount the story changing certain critical details, like the fact that the footballer was dribbling the ball around the other player, but doing so in the shape of a square. This was an attempt to mimic some of the cognitive aspects of lying. Reasonably good liars are often found to base their false accounts partly on things that have actually happened to them, while changing certain core details, rather than making up a completely false account from scratch. As Samuel Butler said: 'The best liar is he who makes the smallest amount of lying go the longest way.' The question was whether the form of the iconic gestures would give some hint as to the real nature of the events at these critical points in the story. The provisional answer seems to be that the iconic gestures often mirror the new false events. Speakers had obviously got the new events firmly in mind when telling the story, but occasionally the original version, the 'true' version, leaked through in their gesture. Thus, one participant narrating the story about the boy dribbling the football said:

and he runs around him [in a square]
Iconic: right hand in space in front of body, index finger straight, other fingers curled, makes a series of anti-clockwise circular movements.

The iconic gesture here still depicted the original 'true' circular movement of the boy and the ball, rather than the changed 'false' version. In other words, the truth seeped through. This experiment is still very much in progress but the provisional results hint at the importance of the precise form of the iconic gestures in determining when people are lying.

Beats would, in all probability, be a good deal simpler to fake than iconic gestures. Indeed there seems to exist good documentary evidence that would attest to this very fact. When Bill Clinton was accused of having sex with Monica Lewinsky, his protestations had quite a number of beats contained within them. Thus:

> BILL CLINTON: <u>I did [not have sexual relations] with that woman, Miss Lewinsky.</u>

Beat: index finger of right hand pointing away from body, other fingers curled up. Hand makes four sharp, rapid downwards movements. Each downward movement begins at the start of each of the four words accompanied by the gesture.

> BILL CLINTON: <u>The allegations (audible swallow) are false (audible swallow)</u>

Beat: fingers on the right hand are straight and apart; hand is positioned vertically to the body. Hand moves downwards twice – first time on the word 'allegations' and second time on the words 'are false'.

However, there is an important point to make here. President Clinton always seemed very determined to use quite a precise language in defending himself during these accusations of sexual misconduct. At the Senate Hearings, President Clinton was asked a series of quite specific questions about his sexual relationship with Monica Lewinsky. The written statement he had provided was that 'These meetings did not consist of sexual intercourse.' He was then asked a series of highly embarrassing, more detailed questions including: 'If Miss Lewinsky says that while you were in the Oval Office area you touched her genitalia would she be lying? That calls for a "yes", "no", or "revert to your former statement".' President Clinton replied: 'I will revert to my statement on that.' He was quite determined to stick to a certain form of words.

During his verbal answers there were quite a few beats actually displayed. So does this mean that he was lying or telling the truth? What he actually said in the Senate Hearings and in a number of interviews at the time is very important here because the words he uses habitually are 'sexual relations' or 'sexual intercourse'. It has since been pointed out to me that there is a saying in the southern states of America that 'eatin' ain't cheatin''. In other words, oral sex does not constitute 'sexual relations'. If President Clinton had managed to persuade himself of the truth of this proposition, then it would allow for the presence of the beats in his speech as an index of truth because he only engaged in oral sex with Miss Lewinsky and not actual sexual intercourse. He might have been using beats in his speech because strictly speaking, in his mind at least, he was actually telling the truth.

Alternatively, of course, it could be that President Clinton was a well-rehearsed liar who had become an expert in the control of most aspects of his body language, except the odd micro-expression in his face and the odd swallow that did slip out rather noticeably on occasion, and that he included the easy to fake beats rather than the more difficult to fake iconic gestures in his speech for effect. Research into the ability of people to fake iconic gestures and beats while they lie is still very much in its infancy, but my bet is that a careful study of these behaviours will always reveal a great deal more than mere attention to speech itself.

So far in this book I have challenged the very notion that some nonverbal behaviour is in any sense separate from language, which has been an assumption underlying a great deal of work in psychology and one of our more general cultural understandings. I have suggested instead that gestures are closely linked to speech and yet present meaning in a form fundamentally different from that of speech. Through hand movements people reveal their inner thoughts and their ways of understanding world events. I have argued that gestures open up a whole new way of regarding thought processes and provide a unique glimpse into how people view the world around them, including the way that they view other people. Gestures, I have argued, can be a window on the human mind and allow us to see thoughts and images that would otherwise be quite invisible. I have offered a glimpse into the thoughts of some of the *Big Brother* housemates as well as into the thoughts of a president of the United States on the spot and in the spotlight.

I should add of course that the academic research on which this book is based is still progressing, so this book reflects work in progress. But my hope is that you, the reader, will now consider those movements of the hands that are made routinely while people talk as at least being worthy of some attention, and not to be dismissed quite as readily as they have been in the past. They are not mere fragments of body language that reflect nervous energy or brief displays of emotion on the part of speakers. They are an integral part of thought itself and very much the other half of language, the neglected half. In the final chapter, I will consider some of the philosophical and practical implications of this new theory.

Some philosophical and practical implications *11*

In this book I have argued, following the pioneering work of David McNeill, that iconic hand gestures are closely linked to speech and yet present meaning in a form fundamentally different from that of speech. Speech is produced sequentially over time and consists of individual words. It is also subject to considerable editorial control as it unfolds gradually through time. Iconic gestures are imagistic, immediate and multidimensional in terms of how meaning is represented and displayed. Through such hand movements, people quite unconsciously and rather unwittingly display their inner thoughts and their ways of understanding events in the world. In the words of David McNeill: 'Gestures are like thoughts themselves.' But unlike thoughts they are highly visible. We can all see them and analyse them, once we have convinced ourselves that they are worthy of some serious consideration in the first place.

This is a very new framework for describing human communication and the relationship between speech and what was traditionally thought of as part of body language. The newness of this position may surprise some readers, who may still be convinced of the utmost superiority of speech over everything else in the communication of meaning. Indeed, they may want to know why language has become the province of speech and not of gesture in all cultures in which hearing is possible. This is a perfectly reasonable question, but was anticipated and answered by Goldin-Meadow and McNeill (1999) in an extremely important paper. They review the evidence of children learning to use language where only signing is possible and conclude: 'If exposed to language in the manual modality [a signed language] children will learn that language as quickly and effortlessly as they learn a spoken language.' In other words, children are born with the potential to learn either a sign language or a spoken language with roughly comparable ease. Why then is the world full of cultures where speaking is the norm rather than signing? The obvious answer to this question is that speech triumphed over any sign languages because it is simply so good at delivering messages in a segmented and combinatorial form, with words and syntax combining to deliver meaning. Goldin-Meadow and McNeill argue that sign languages are just as good at this. They suggest a different explanation, a completely radical explanation as to why speech triumphed over manual language, with a very different perspective on the evolution of human communication. They argue that speech is used to deliver the basic segmented and combinatorial code 'not because of its strengths but to compensate for its weaknesses'. Think of some of those examples again.

and he [bends it way back]
Iconic: hand appears to grip something and pull it from the upper front space back and down near to the shoulder.

And she [chases him out again]
Iconic: hand appears to swing an object through the air.

[she's eating the food]
Iconic: fingers on left hand are close together, palm is facing body, and thumb is directly behind index finger. Hand moves from waist level towards mouth.

the head starts [swimming] along
Iconic: right hand indicates the way that the head is swimming in the water, focusing on forward motion with splayed fingers representing the head.

bouncing the ball [on the ground]
Iconic: palm of right hand points downwards; hand moves rapidly downwards and upwards three times.

and the [roof starts cracking]
Iconic: index finger of left hand points vertically upwards, other fingers and thumb are slightly curled. Index finger moves to his left and then to his right.

Speech conveys the meaning in each of these cases by a rule-governed combination of words. The iconic gesture conveys meaning through the images created spontaneously and unconsciously by the speaker. Think of the images created by the speaker in each of the above cases and just consider once again the way that they complement the information conveyed in the speech. Both speech and gesture refer to the same event in each case but the speech and the gesture each present a somewhat different aspect of it. Of course, the extraordinary thing is that although gesture and speech represent meaning in different ways the two form a single integrated system, precisely timed as we have seen, significantly more effective than either on its own.

I have spent a number of chapters in this book demonstrating the power of this single integrated system, reviewing a number of experiments that have shown conclusively that gesture–speech combinations are more powerful than either speech or gesture on their own. Once you accept some of these basic premises, Goldin-Meadow and McNeill's (1999) conclusions become slightly less startling. They build their argument: 'While both gesture and speech are able to assume a segmented and combinatorial format, only gesture is well suited to the imagistic format.' This leads on to the inevitable conclusion, which I will quote verbatim because of its importance to how we construe human communication and its evolution:

> If our hypothesis is correct, speech became the predominant medium of human language not because it is so well suited to the segmented and combinatorial requirements of symbolic communication (the manual modality is equally suited to the job) but rather because it is not particularly good at capturing the mimectic components of

human communication (a task at which the manual
modality excels).

(Goldin-Meadow and McNeill 1999: 166)

In other words, according to Goldin-Meadow and McNeill
we all ended up speaking rather than signing in the natural
state to keep our hands free to create the spontaneous
images that we do during everyday talk. We could, of
course, have ended up using manual signs instead as the
basic form of communication, but this would have been less
effective because the speech modality is nowhere near as
good at creating images to help the communication along.

This is an extraordinary view of the evolution of human
language and communication, but it does have considerable
merit when you consider the evidence presented in this
book. The argument completely subverts Hewes' argument
that language evolved from gesture and the 'gesture did not
wither away, but persisted as a common accompaniment to
speech' (1973/1992: 71). Rather than not merely withering
away, Goldin-Meadow and McNeill suggest that it was to
keep gesture flourishing that speech developed in the way
that it did.

I find this new theory of human evolution intriguing and
strangely compelling; compelling because it recognizes the
huge scale of what iconic gestures do in everyday life. The
obvious objection to the new theory, which is that speech is
simply more efficient than manual signing as the basic form
of communication because it can be produced faster and
over greater distances than any sign language, is not as
conclusive as you might think when you consider the claims
of people like McBride who argues: 'Aborigines find signing
faster than speaking and more effective at distances, and
some groups find it more elegant than speech' (1973: 75).

If you accept some of the evidence presented in this book,
then you may have to rethink many of the most basic
assumptions about the nature of human communication;
about the separation of language and body language and
about why speech became the primary vehicle of human
communication. You will also have to rethink some very

deeply held beliefs about the functions of language and the nonverbal system of communication. It is a widespread belief that language is linked to thinking and to communicating information about the world and that nonverbal communication has quite different emotional and relationship functions. But now this deeply held view seems not to be correct.

I used an example towards the start of Chapter 2 that I now wish to return to. To demonstrate this traditional view, I stated that 'It will rain tomorrow in Manchester, again' is easily conveyed by language but not at all easily conveyed by nonverbal communication. I tried to do this consciously and deliberately at the time but I couldn't quite capture 'tomorrow', 'Manchester' or 'again' using nonverbal communication, although I could manage 'rain'. So how can I explain this failure in the light of the new theory that I have outlined in this book? The point is, of course, that iconic hand gestures and speech have evolved to work together to communicate the full intended meaning. Speech conveys much of the meaning in this example, but there is still a lot left for the iconic gesture to do. The iconic movement accompanying this sentence, my fingers pitter-pattering downwards, would convey not just the concept of 'rain' but also additional information about how hard the rain falls in Manchester (forceful pitter-pattering suggesting heavy rain) and how persistent the rain is (the pitter-pattering movement would probably co-occur with the entire sentence suggesting very persistent rain – it never stops raining in Manchester, trust me!). That is how the two systems work. The speaker never needs to say verbally how hard or how persistent the rain is in Manchester. The iconic gesture does that for him or her. I tried to use nonverbal communication for the whole message in Chapter 2, which is why I failed. If I had said this sentence spontaneously at the time, then the iconic gesture would almost certainly have slipped into my communication with great ease and considerable effectiveness.

However, there is another major implication of this work. If you accept the evidence that I have presented then you will also have to change how you behave in everyday life.

There is no such thing any longer as being merely a good listener. You will have to watch speakers that much more carefully if you really want to understand what others are thinking. This is because not only do iconic and metaphoric gestures communicate significant amounts of information, but it is not at all clear that such communication is under the same degree of conscious control and editing as speech itself. Iconic and metaphoric gestures are like parts of unedited thinking and can therefore potentially be enormously revealing. They should never be ignored.

There are also, of course, a number of possible practical applications of this research. If the human brain has evolved to deal with both speech and gesture, with both the auditory-vocal and the visual systems of communication simultaneously, then this might have significant implications for the effectiveness of communications that rely on both systems of communication as opposed to just one or the other. Again to quote David McNeill: 'Utterances possess two sides, only one of which is speech; the other is imagery, actional and visuo-spatial. To exclude the gesture side, as has been traditional, is tantamount to ignoring half of the message out of the brain.' (2000: 139).

Heather Shovelton and I have repeatedly demonstrated (Beattie and Shovelton 1999a, 1999b, 2001a) that when experimental participants have available both sides of the message, the speech and the gesture, they obtain significantly more information about whatever domain is being discussed. But what are the implications of this for something like advertising in which the effectiveness of communication is paramount?

This was the very question put to me by Jim Hytner, Marketing Director of ITV, whom I met quite by chance at a conference, and who then put me in touch with Fran Cassidy, Marketing Director of Carlton Television, Tony Hopewell-Smith, Research Director of Carlton Television and Adrian Ebery, Broadcast Research Controller of Carlton Television. They challenged me to put this new theory to the test. Their interest was pretty clear. If I could demonstrate that mixed messages containing speech and image (in the form of iconic gesture) were significantly more powerful in terms of communication than linguistic messages on their own, either in the form of speech messages (radio) or text (newspapers), then television in general and ITV in particular would be fairly happy. This was especially so because television advertising seems to have been under sustained attack from these other media who were claiming that the effectiveness of television as a medium could not justify the costs involved in television advertising. The feeling in television and in advertising generally was that television commercials were more effective – but how much more effective? Perhaps even more importantly, why might television be more effective as a medium of communication?

What was interesting about the research being done at Manchester was that we were able to quantify the amount of information transmitted by speech on its own compared with the mixed messages containing both speech and gesture. In addition, what we were also doing of course was following the work of David McNeill. We were developing a theory of why this might be so. Carlton Television was keen to determine if the kinds of experiments that Heather Shovelton and I had been doing on cartoon stories applied to anything in the real world like advertising. We of course were keen to take up their challenge.

The methodology was quite simple. We developed three product descriptions for a car, a holiday and a mobile phone. These descriptions were what you might call proto-advertisements. They were fairly basic commercial messages extolling the virtues of the three products. The most basic was the text version, the basic script for the proto-advertisement. Then we recorded an audio version (like a radio advertisement) in which one male and one female actor delivered the script. Next we recorded a video version where we wrote a detailed specification for six iconic gestures for each product to be generated during the delivery of the message (with 18 iconic gestures in total in the three messages). This detailed specification identified both the form of the gestures and the exact timing of each gesture; i.e. exactly where the iconic gesture should start and finish with respect to the verbal message, and also the span of the individual iconic gestures in the gestural space, which is the area in front of the body where the trajectory of the gesture occurs. These three parameters of the gestures – their form, their timing and their span in the gestural space – derived from a pilot investigation of 50 participants who were filmed describing these same three products. We were interested in the kinds of iconic gestures that people use spontaneously and naturally when talking about cars, holidays and mobile phones. We wanted to discover exactly how these iconic gestures would be executed. We then developed a series of six questions per product to determine what information each participant, who was presented with one of the three versions of the message, obtained from each of the communications.

The basic scripts and the iconic gestures that were inserted into the scripts are detailed below. Note how some of the iconic gestures add information that is not in the text version and some merely emphasize information that already exists in the underlying script.

The same fundamental psychological question arises as in the first study that Heather Shovelton and I conducted in this area (Beattie and Shovelton 1999a): does the human brain respond to both the linguistic channel and the imagistic gestural channel and somehow combine the information from both channels, or do human beings socialized and schooled in the primacy of language focus exclusively (or mainly) on the linguistic channel in the communication of semantic information? Semantic information is the key term here. We are not dealing with the emotional content of the advertisement (something that is no doubt very important). We are interested in the actual semantic information about the actual product – 'how smooth the flight is'; 'how quickly the car accelerates'; 'what happens to the indicators when the car is travelling quickly'; 'what proportion of the time it is sunny on the beach in the holiday destination'; 'how safe the sea is'; 'how big the mobile phone is'; 'how the mobile phone vibrates'. In terms of the questionnaire there were four possible responses for each question and each response was scored unambiguously as either correct or incorrect. The full texts of the advertisements, with the accompanying iconic gestures, are outlined below.

Holiday

Beach Holidays Ltd is a new holiday company designed to help you get the kind of relaxing beach holiday we all dream of.

All our holiday destinations are situated in extremely beautiful locations and yet they are only a [short flight] away.
Right hand is by the side of the head; fingers are close together and palm is pointing downwards; hand moves horizontally away from the head in a rapid, short, steady movement.

You can relax and sunbathe on long golden beaches, where there is a [clear blue sky and the sun is out].
Right hand is in a vertical position; fingers are pointing straight upwards; hand moves in a straight line from the left to the right. Hand then stops and fingers move apart. Fingers then curl up before stretching open again and this is repeated three times.

If you need to cool down you can go [swimming] in the sea
Hands are touching at the front of the body; hands and arms move slowly forward away from the body. Hands and arms then move slowly away from each other, before beginning to come together again so that a slow circular motion is made by each arm.

and you needn't worry about the children as the sea is particularly [safe] in the holiday destinations we choose, plus there are 24-hour-
Right hand is in front of the body; palm is pointing downwards. Hand moves slowly to the right and produces very slight, smooth, up and down movements as it is does so.

a-day lifeguards. In fact your only worry will be what factor suntan cream to put on. You will be able to [eat local delicacies], which
Right hand is in front of body, palm is pointing upwards; fingers and thumb are slightly curled. Hand then moves towards the mouth, it then remains there for a second, before returning to a position in front of the body.

are cheap yet of good quality. You can wander around markets and observe the local customs.

If you wish you [can dance the night away]
Both arms are bent at the elbows. Right hand is slightly curved and above the head; left hand is slightly curved and is in area in front of the thighs. The two hands then swap positions before returning to their original position.

or you can continue to relax and enjoy the entertainment we provide for you.

We are sure that any holiday with Beach Holidays Ltd will be a dream come true.

Car

The new BS is a car right at the top of its league. It performs amazingly in every weather condition. It has anti-lock brakes therefore the BS has the ability to [stop very quickly], even in the wettest or iciest conditions.
Left hand moves very rapidly from the right to the left then stops extremely abruptly in the area in front of the body.

The [speed of acceleration] that the BS is capable of is truly magnificent
Left hand is horizontal with palm pointing upwards. Right hand is also horizontal but palm is pointing downwards. Right hand moves rapidly over the left hand and away from the body. The left hand remains stationary.

and it can handle sharp bends and uneven roads beautifully.

The BS is well equipped for the summer months as it comes with air conditioning and an easy to use electric sunroof.

The BS has a top of the range CD player and stunning [alloy wheels] that
Hands are wide apart in front of the body; palms are pointing towards each other and fingers are wide open and slightly curved.

come as standard.

Safety features include new style [effective airbags]
Hands move upwards towards the face; fingers are close together and palms are pointing towards the face. Hands stop moving when they reach the area just in front of the face and fingers move apart. [Person is smiling!]

and a perfect view, for the driver, of what is happening around the outside of the car.

A final revolutionary safety feature is that the indicators [get louder] the faster
Hands move repeatedly towards each other until they are touching and then away from each other so that a clapping motion occurs. The sound produced is quiet to start with and gradually becomes louder and louder.

the car is travelling so that they can be heard on roads such as motorways.

All in all, the BS has a beautiful appearance and performs amazingly without sacrificing safety or value for money. In fact you get all this for an amazingly [reasonable price] of twelve thousand pounds.
Left arm is stretched down by the side of the body; palm of hand is pointing towards the floor. Hand makes sharp movement to the left and then to the right.

Mobile phone

The new Diva mobile phone is the phone for the future. It allows you to have internet access yet it is still [compact] and stylish.
Palm of right hand is pointing upwards; thumb and index finger are about four centimetres away from each other.

It can be used cheaply whilst travelling abroad, so you will be able to [remain in contact] with people wherever you are.
Right hand and arm is stretched upwards above the head; left hand and arm is stretched downwards by the left side of the body. Hands move towards each other and meet in front of the body. Fingers on the right hand link with the fingers on the left hand. This position is held for three seconds before the hands move apart again and return to their original position.

The [loudness of the ring] and the type of ring tone can be varied to suit

Index finger of right hand is about 10 centimetres away from the right-hand side of the head. Finger moves towards the ear making small up and down movements, finger then moves back to its original position. This is repeated four times.

your location, so whether you're at a pop concert or having a quiet walk in the country the volume of the ring will be perfect. Even the silent coaches on trains are catered for as you can set the phone to remain silent but [vibrate]

Palm of right hand is pointing upwards; thumb and index finger are about four centimetres away from each other. Hand produces small rapid movements from side to side.

when somebody calls you.

And then you always have the option of whether to reply using a rapid, simple [text message].

Palm of left hand is pointing upwards; fingers are together and slightly curved. Index finger of right hand is stretched out and is moving from side to side just above the palm of the left hand. Fingers of the right hand move together and then make a rapid flick away from the body.

The new Diva phone comes with a hands-free kit so that it is [safe to use even in the car].

Hands are both in front of the chest; fingers and thumbs are curled up, so that each hand makes a circle, as if a steering wheel is being held. As the right hand moves upwards the left hand moves downwards and as the left hand moves upwards the right hand moves downwards. [The person is also talking away happily.]

The Diva phone makes keeping in contact hassle free, fun and affordable.

We used 150 participants in the first study; 50 participants in each independent group responded to each of the three messages, but only in one medium. In other words, the same 50 participants responded to the video version for all three products, and likewise for the speech and text-only versions. To give you a specific example of the kinds of semantic information tapped by the questionnaire, consider the following. The message about the holiday company included the sentence 'You will be able to eat local delicacies, which are cheap yet of good quality.' The accompanying gesture was as follows: *'Right hand is in front of body, palm is pointing upwards; fingers and thumb are slightly curled. Hand then moves towards the mouth, it then remains there for a second, before returning to a position in front of the body.'* The corresponding question, which the experimental participants had to answer once they had received the whole message, was: 'How will you eat the local delicacies?' (a) with a knife and fork; (b) with a spoon; (c) with your hand; (d) with chopsticks. The correct answer here was (c) and the information required correctly to answer this question was only in the gesture, not in the speech. In the case of 12 questions (out of a total of 18) the information required was represented most fully by the speech–gesture combinations.

In the case of the other six questions (randomly distributed across the three products) all of the information required to answer the question correctly was in the speech. The gesture merely emphasized this information.

There are a few important details to include of how this experiment was carried out. The messages were delivered in a random order. Those participants in the audio condition were played exactly the same tapes as those in the video but without the vision channel, thus only the sound could be heard. Participants in the text condition read the transcripts of the speech only. They were allowed to spend up to one minute reading the transcripts because this is the approximate length of time that each narration actually took. All of the participants were run in groups of approximately 25. Some of the video and audio groups received the female actor delivering the message, whereas others received the male actor delivering the message. After each message had been played or read, the participant immediately filled in the corresponding questionnaire. The same questionnaires were given to the participants in the three different presentation conditions.

The results were striking. It was found that significantly more questions were answered correctly in the video condition than in either the audio or text condition and that there was no significant difference between the text and audio conditions.

The actual figures obtained make interesting reading. Let's remind ourselves that as each of the 18 questions have 4 alternative answers, participants will obtain an average of 4.50 correct answers, out of a maximum of 18, simply due to chance. This has to be taken into account when assessing the amount of information communicated by the message in each of the conditions. In the case of the video condition the increase from chance to the actual number of correct answers obtained is 5.98 (10.48 minus 4.50); for the audio condition it is 4.18 (8.68 minus 4.50); and for the text condition it is 4.32 (8.82 minus 4.50). Therefore the participants in the video condition gain 43 per cent more information than the participants in the audio condition and 38 per cent more information than those participants in the text condition (Figure 11.1).

FIGURE 11.1. The percentage increase in correct answers when moving from the audio condition to the text and video conditions.

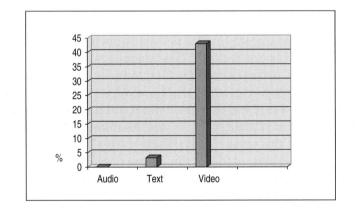

This increase afforded by the video condition (speech plus gesture), however, is substantially greater in the case of certain products, in particular the holiday company in which there was an enormous increase in communicative effectiveness in the video condition. As there were 6 questions about each product and each question has 4 alternative answers, participants will obtain an average of 1.5 correct answers simply due to chance in this case on any particular product. When participants receive the video message about the holiday, the increase from chance to the actual number of correct answers obtained is 2.36; for the audio condition it is 1.12; for the text condition it is 1.04. Therefore the participants in the video condition gain 111 per cent more information about the holiday company than the participants in the audio condition and 127 per cent more information about the holiday company than those participants in the text condition (Figure 11.2).

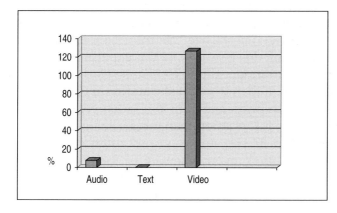

FIGURE 11.2.
The percentage increase in correct answers about the holiday company, when moving from the text condition to the audio and video conditions.

Next we investigated whether or not the knowledge that people already possess about a product affects the amount of information obtained from the different presentation conditions. For example, we would assume (in a somewhat sexist way, I do admit) that the car is a product which in general men would probably know more about than women. When we conducted the analysis we found that after chance was again taken into account the increase from the audio condition to the video condition for men answering questions about a car was 64 per cent, whereas for women the increase was 166 per cent. In other words, the gestures present in the video condition seem to communicate most to those who have least knowledge about a particular product (Figure 11.3).

But what happens with respect to information that is

FIGURE 11.3.
The percentage
increase in correct
answers about the
car, when moving
from the audio
condition to the video
condition, for males
and females.

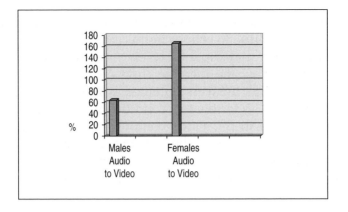

already fully displayed in the speech itself, where the gesture can merely emphasize this information? This was the case for six of the gestures in the experiment. Even here significantly more questions were answered correctly in the video condition than in either the audio condition or the text condition. The participants in the video condition gain 23 per cent more information than the participants in the audio condition and 32 per cent more information than those in the text condition, even when all of the semantic information is explicit in the verbal message.

This research had now finally come out of the world of cartoons and the *Big Brother* household and had ended up very much in the hard commercial world of advertising. It demonstrated conclusively that television messages are significantly more effective at conveying information than either audio messages (radio) or text messages (newspapers). It managed to quantify this effectiveness and suggest a good reason in terms of a new theory of human communication and the evolution of human communication why this might be so. But as usual in research more questions arose immediately, now with a commercial edge to them. Why were some of the iconic gestures more effective than others? Suddenly the advertisers wanted to know and this was no longer merely an academic question. Preliminary analyses suggested that the most effective iconic gestures in these proto-advertisements (the most effective gestures operationally defined as greater than the median in terms of measured effectiveness) were quite large gestures with a large span. We found a significant statistical effect between the communicative effectiveness of the individual gesture and the number of boundary lines crossed in the gestural space (the area in front of the speaker in which gestures are made). This can be seen in Figure 11.4 where the start point of each gesture (marked by an X) and the end point of each gesture (marked by an O) are indicated. The boundary lines are the unbroken lines representing squares or rectangles around the body (the diagram is derived from McNeill 1992). The least effective gestures were those with a very small span which were probably less well noticed in the actual experiment (Figure 11.5).

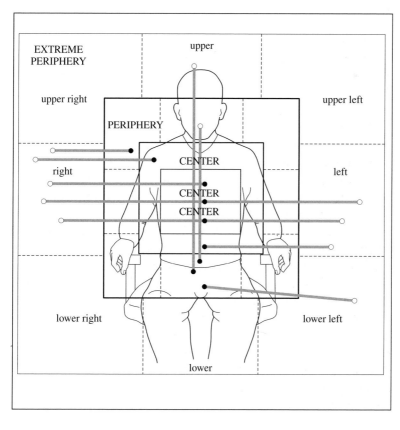

FIGURE 11.4.
The space used by those gestures found to be most effective in communication. X = start point of gesture, O = end point of gesture.

FIGURE 11.5.
The space used by
those gestures found
to be least effective
in communication. X
= start point of
gesture, O = end
point of gesture.

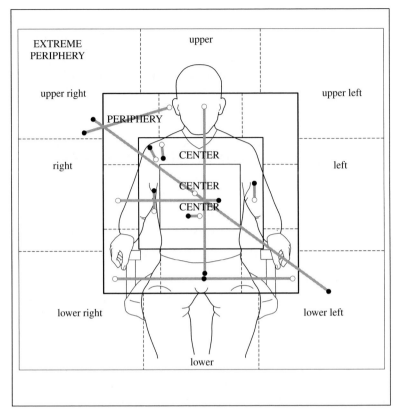

The excitement that these results generated was considerable and I presented two major talks based on this work, one at the British Museum in November 2002 and one in Budapest in December 2002 in front of hard-bitten cynical media researchers, 'creatives' and budget directors from advertising agencies, who seemed (at times almost reluctantly) to be quite taken with this new theory of human communication. The analyses continued and I subsequently demonstrated that when the proto-advertisements were played repeatedly to sets of participants, the audio and text versions never closed the gap on the video version across five trials. The video actually increased its effectiveness by 25 per cent across the 5 trials, the audio by 20 per cent and the text by 18 per cent. This can be seen in Figure 11.6.

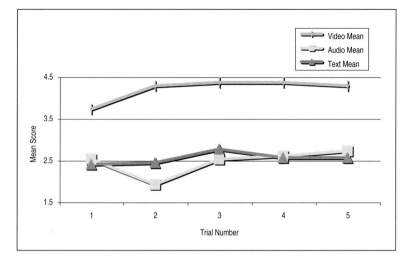

FIGURE 11.6.
The mean scores obtained for all five trials for the video, audio and text versions.

In addition, the participants seemed to remember the video messages better than either of the other two types of message three months after the first exposure when the same questionnaire was readministered. This latter observation would not really have surprised Aristotle. The video version does after all involve both speech and imagery and orators in ancient Greece used imagery-based mnemonic techniques to memorize speeches. It would also not have surprised some cognitive psychologists like Paivio (1969, 1971, 1986), who has proposed two basic independent but interconnected coding or symbolic systems for human cognition: a nonverbal system, which works with images, and a verbal system, which works with words and propositions. Paivio has maintained that both systems are specialized for encoding, organizing, storing and retrieving distinct types of information, but that the two systems are interconnected and can produce additive effects. In this experiment with iconic gestures and speech we see considerable evidence of these additive effects in action.

But I think that there is an additional point really worth emphasizing over and above the fact that gesture–speech communications are remembered better. In this experiment I studied the kinds of natural images that are generated alongside speech. In other words, in everyday natural communication speakers spontaneously generate images to accompany their talk. Thereby through this activity they are helping to encode the content of speech into the memory of another person. The ancient Greeks did recognize the power of imagery and the rhetorical role of stylized gestures in oratory, but perhaps they underestimated the power of *spontaneous* iconic gesture in communication and in everyday life.

Of course, the requirements of media researchers trying to justify their budgets are always going to be different from that of theoretical psychologists. My ongoing research in this area considers real advertisements and not just proto-advertisements, advertisements made with all the skill that creatives in advertising agencies can provide; advertisements that affect both our mood and emotion, advertisements that create a need within us for the product and somehow compel us to spend money, and sometimes even money that we haven't got. These advertisements will involve not just iconic gestures but other types of skilful image as well. This new research is very much driven by core psychological concerns – research into the very nature of human communication on the relationship between the verbal and the nonverbal systems and speculation, from an evolutionary perspective, about how and why we all ended up speaking (and gesturing) rather than merely gesturing.

Hopefully in this book I have taken the reader on some sort of journey; a journey that started in established psychological orthodoxy and in the traditional psychological laboratory but moved outside that to less familiar territories. The work took a fresh look at some old issues. It zigzagged out of the laboratory and even ended up in the *Big Brother* house where some new insights into human social interaction, and the underlying mechanisms, were being made available. The story ends temporarily in Soho, central London, in the flashy new advertising agencies with men with short spiky hair, black designer glasses and short no-nonsense names – Don, Al, Jon – desperate to understand the full significance of this new perspective to impress their female boss. I suspect that the journey and the excitement is not quite over yet; at least I hope that it's not over for me or for my colleagues.

I started this latest wave of research with Heather Shovelton who is now a Simon Research Fellow at the University of Manchester and we both followed warily in the footsteps of others. I have been interested in iconic gesture off and on since I was a student at Cambridge and for that I must thank Brian Butterworth who introduced me to this area in the first place. But I know myself that I would not have got excited about this area of research for a second time if it had not been for the pioneering work of David McNeill and especially his book *Hand and Mind*. Quite simply it was one of those seminal books brimming with insight and new ideas. David McNeill retires from teaching in 2003 and it seems extremely appropriate that I dedicate the present work to him.

References

Aarsleff, H. (ed.) (2001) *Condillac: Essay on the Origin of Human Knowledge*, Cambridge: Cambridge University Press.

Aboudan, R. and Beattie, G. (1996) 'Cross-cultural similarities in gestures: The deep relationship between gestures and speech, which transcend language barriers', *Semiotica* 111: 269–94.

Argyle, M. (1972) *The Psychology of Interpersonal Behaviour*, 2nd edn, London: Penguin.

Argyle, M., Alkema, F. and Gilmour, R. (1971) 'The communication of friendly and hostile attitudes by verbal and nonverbal signals', *European Journal of Social Psychology* 1: 385–402.

Argyle, M., Salter, V., Nicholson, H., Williams, M. and Burgess, P. (1970) 'The communication of inferior and superior attitudes by verbal and nonverbal signals', *British Journal of Social and Clinical Psychology* 9: 222–31.

Argyle, M. and Trower, P. (1979) *Person to Person: Ways of Communicating*, London: Harper and Row.

Austin, G. (1806/1966) *Chironomia or, a Treatise on Rhetorical Delivery*, Carbondale and Edwardsville: Southern Illinois University Press.

Bacon, F. (1605/1952) *The Advancement of Learning. Great Books of the Western World, Volume 30, Francis Bacon*, Chicago: Encyclopedia Britannica.

Barakat, R. (1973) 'Arabic gestures', *Journal of Popular Culture* 6: 749–87.

Bates, E. (1976) *Language and Context*, New York: Academic Press.

Bates, E., Benigni, L., Bretherton, I., Camaioni, L. and Volterra, V. (1979) *The Emergence of Symbols: Cognition and Communication in Infancy*, New York: Academic Press.

Bateson, G. (1968) 'Redundancy and coding', in T. Sebeok (ed.) *Animal Communication*, Bloomington: Indiana University Press, pp. 614–26.

Beattie, G. (1983) *Talk: An Analysis of Speech and Nonverbal Behaviour in Conversation*, Milton Keynes: Open University Press.

Beattie, G. and Aboudan, R. (1994) 'Gestures, pauses and speech: An experimental investigation of the effects of changing social context on their precise temporal relationships', *Semiotica* 99: 239–72.

Beattie, G. and Coughlan, J. (1998) 'Do iconic gestures have a functional role in lexical access? An experimental study of the effects of repeating a verbal message on gesture production', *Semiotica* 119: 221–49.

—— (1999) 'An experimental investigation of the role of iconic gestures in lexical access using the tip-of-the-tongue phenomenon', *British Journal of Psychology* 90: 35–56.

Beattie, G. and Shovelton, H. (1998) 'The communicational significance of the iconic hand gestures which accompany spontaneous speech: An experimental and critical appraisal', in S. Santi, I. Guaitella, C. Cave and G. Konopczynski (eds) *Oralité et gestualité communication multimodale, interaction*, Paris: L'Harmattan, pp. 371–5.

—— (1999a) 'Do iconic hand gestures really contribute anything to the semantic information conveyed by speech? An experimental investigation', *Semiotica* 123: 1–30.

—— (1999b) 'Mapping the range of information contained in the iconic hand gestures that accompany spontaneous speech', *Journal of Language and Social Psychology* 18: 438–62.

—— (2000) 'Iconic hand gestures and the predictability of words in context in spontaneous speech', *British Journal of Psychology* 91: 473–92.

—— (2001a) 'An experimental investigation of the role of different types of iconic gesture in communication: A semantic feature approach', *Gesture* 1: 129–49.

—— (2001b) 'How gesture viewpoint influences what information decoders receive from iconic gestures', in C. Cave, I. Guaitella and S. Santi (eds) *Oralité et gestualité: Interactions et comportements multimodaux dans la communication*, Paris: L'Harmattan, pp. 283–7.

—— (2002a) 'What properties of talk are associated with the generation of spontaneous iconic hand gestures?', *British Journal of Social Psychology* 41: 403–17.

—— (2002b) 'An experimental investigation of some properties of individual iconic gestures that affect their communicative power', *British Journal of Psychology* 93: 473–92.

—— (2002c) 'Lexical access in talk: A critical consideration of transitional probability and word frequency as possible determinants of pauses in spontaneous speech', *Semiotica* 141: 49–71.

Birdwhistell, R. L. (1970) *Kinesics and Context: Essays on Body Motion Communication*, Philadelphia: University of Pennsylvania Press.

Bond, C., Kahler, K. and Paolicelli, L. (1985) 'The miscommunication of deception: An adaptive perspective', *Journal of Experimental Social Psychology* 21: 331–45.

Brown, A. S. (1991) 'A review of the tip-of-the-tongue experience', *Psychological Bulletin* 109: 204–23.

Brown, R. and McNeill, D. (1966) 'The "tip of the tongue" phenomenon', *Journal of Verbal Learning and Verbal Behaviour* 5: 325–37.

Bulwer, J. (1644/1974) *Chirologia: Or the Natural Language of the Hand and Chironomia: Or the Art of Manual Rhetoric*. Carbondale, IL: Southern Illinois University Press.

Butler. S. (1903) *The Way of All Flesh*, London: Methuen.

Butterworth, B. and Hadar, U. (1989) 'Gesture, speech, and computational stages: A reply to McNeill', *Psychological Review* 96: 168–74.

Chomsky, N. (1957) *Syntactic Structures*, The Hague: Mouton.

—— (1972) *Language and Mind*. New York: Harcourt Brace.

—— (1976) *Reflections on Language*. London: Temple Smith.

Church, R. B. and Goldin-Meadow, S. (1986) 'The mismatch between gesture and speech an index of transitional knowledge', *Cognition* 23: 43–71.

Cody, M. and O'Hair, H. (1983) 'Nonverbal communication and deception: Differences in deception cues due to gender and communicator dominance', *Communication Monographs* 50: 175–93.

Condillac, E. B. de (1756/2001) *An Essay on the Origin of Human Knowledge*. Cambridge: Cambridge University Press.

Darwin, C. (1859/1971) *The Origin of Species*, London: Dent

—— (1872) *The Expression of the Emotions in Man and Animals*. London: John Murray.

Davis, M. and Hadiks, D. (1995) 'Demeanor and credibility', *Semiotica* 106: 5–54.

deTurck, M. and Miller, G. (1985) 'Deception and arousal: Isolating the behavioral correlates of deception', *Human Communication Research* 12: 181–201.

Diderot, D. (1751/1916) *'Lettre sur les sourds et muets'*, in H. Jourdain (ed.) (trans.) *Diderot's Early Philosophical Works*, Chicago: Open Court Publishing.

Efron, D. (1941/1972) *Gesture and Environment*, New York: King's Crown Press.

Ekman, P. (1985) *Telling Lies: Clues to Deceit in the Marketplace, Politics, and Marriage*, London: Norton.

—— (1988) 'Lying and nonverbal behavior: Theoretical issues and new findings', *Journal of Nonverbal Behavior* 12: 163–76.

Ekman, P. and Friesen, W. (1969) 'The repertoire of nonverbal behavioural categories: Origins, usage, and coding', *Semiotica* 1: 49–98.

Ekman, P. and Friesen, W. (1972) 'Hand movements', *Journal of Communication* 22: 353–74.

Ekman, P., Friesen, W. and Scherer, K. (1976) 'Body movement and voice pitch in deceptive interaction', *Semiotica* 16: 23–7.

Ekman, P., O'Sullivan, M., Friesen, W. and Scherer, K. (1991) 'Face, voice, and body in detecting deceit', *Journal of Nonverbal Behavior* 15: 125–35.

Ellis, A. and Beattie, G. (1986) *The Psychology of Language and Communication*, New York: Guilford Press.

Freud, S. (1905/1953) 'Fragments of an analysis of a case of hysteria', in *Standard Edition of the Complete Psychological Works of Sigmund Freud, Vol. 7*, London: Hogarth Press.

Gardner, A. and Gardner, B. T. (1978) 'Comparative psychology and language acquisition', in K. Saltzinger and F. L. Denmark (eds) *Psychology: The State of the Art. Annals of the New York Academy of Sciences, Vol. 309*, New York: New York Academy of Sciences.

Goldin-Meadow, S. (1999) 'The development of gesture with and without speech in hearing and deaf children', in L. Messing and R. Campbell (eds) *Gesture, Speech and Sign*, Oxford: Oxford University Press, pp. 117–32.

Goldin-Meadow, S. and McNeill, D. (1999) 'The role of gesture and mimetic representation in making language the province of speech', in M. Corballis and S. Lea (eds) *The Descent of Mind*, Oxford: Oxford University Press, pp. 155–72.

Goldin-Meadow, S., McNeill, D. and Singleton, J. (1996) 'Silence is liberating: Removing the handcuffs on grammatical expression in the manual modality', *Psychological Review* 103: 34–55.

Goldman-Eisler, F. (1968) *Psycholinguistics: Experiments in Spontaneous Speech*, London: Academic Press.

Greene, J., O'Hair, H., Cody, M. and Yen, C. (1985) 'Planning and control of behavior during deception', *Human Communication Research* 11: 335–64.

Hadar, U. (2001) 'The recognition of the meaning of ideational gestures by untrained subjects', in C. Cave, I. Guaitella and S. Santi (eds) *Oralité et gestualité: interactions et comportements multimodaux dans la communication*, Paris: L'Harmattan, pp. 292–5.

Hall, E. T. (1959) *The Silent Language*, Garden City: Doubleday.

Hewes, G. (1973a) 'Primate communication and the gestural origin of language', *Current Anthropology* 14: 5–12.

—— (1973b) 'Reply to critics', *Current Anthropology* 14: 19–21.

—— (1992) 'Primate communication and

the gestural origin of language', *Current Anthropology* 33(suppl.): 65–84.

Hockett, C. (1960) 'The origin of speech', *Scientific American* 203: 88–96.

—— (1978) 'In search of Jove's brow', *American Speech* 53: 243–313.

Hofer, E., Kohnken, G., Hanewinkel, R. and Bruhn, C. (1993) *Diagnostik und Attribution von Glaubwürdigkeit*. Final report to the Deutsche Forschungsgemeinschaft, KO 882/4-2, Kiel: University of Kiel.

James, W. (1893) *The Principles of Psychology*, vol. 1. New York: Holt.

Jancovic, M. A., Devoe, S. and Wiener, M. (1975) 'Age-related changes in hand and arm movements as nonverbal communication: Some conceptualisations and an empirical exploration', *Child Development* 46: 922–8.

Kalma, A., Witte, M. and Zaalberg, R. (1996) Authenticity: Operationalization, manipulation, and behavioural components: An explanation', *Medium Psychologie* 8: 49–65.

Kendon, A. (1972) 'Some relationships between body motion and speech', in A. Siegman and B. Pope (eds) *Studies in Dyadic Communication*, New York: Pergamon Press, pp. 177–210.

—— (1980) 'Gesticulation and speech: Two aspects of the process of utterance', in M. R. Key (ed.) *The Relation between Verbal and Nonverbal Communication*, The Hague: Mouton, pp. 207–27.

—— (1982) 'The study of gesture: Some observations on its history', *Semiotic Inquiry* 2: 45–62.

—— (1988) 'How gestures can become like words', in F. Poyatos (ed.) *Cross-cultural Perspectives in Nonverbal Communication*, Toronto: Hogrefe, pp. 131–41.

Kennedy, G. (1972) *The Art of Rhetoric in the Roman World: 300BC–AD300*. Princeton: Princeton University Press.

Kortlandt, A. (1973) 'Comment on Hewes', *Current Anthropology* 14: 13–14.

—— (1992) 'Comment on Hewes', *Current Anthropology* 33(suppl.): 73–74.

Krauss, R., Morrel-Samuels, P. and Colasante, C. (1991) 'Do conversational hand gestures communicate?', *Journal of Personality and Social Psychology* 61: 743–54.

La Barre, Weston (1964) 'Paralinguistics, kinesics, and cultural anthropology', in T. A. Sebeok (ed.) *Approaches to Semiotics*, The Hague: Mouton, pp. 191–220.

Laing, R. D. and Esterson, A. (1964) *Sanity, Madness and the Family*, London: Penguin.

Lee, V. and Beattie, G. (1998) 'The rhetorical organisation of verbal and nonverbal behaviour in emotion talk', *Semiotica* 120: 39–92.

Leroi-Gourhan, A. (1964–65) *Le Geste et la Parole*, 2 vols, Paris: Albin Marcel.

Levelt, W. J. M. (ed.) (1993) *Lexical Access in Speech Production*, Cambridge, MA: Blackwell.

McBride, G. (1973) 'Comment on Hewes', *Current Anthropology* 14: 13–14.

Maclay, H. and Osgood, C. E. (1959) 'Hesitation phenomena in spontaneous English speech', *Word* 15: 19–44.

McNeill, D. (1985) 'So you think gestures are nonverbal?', *Psychological Review* 92: 350–71.

—— (1992) *Hand and Mind. What Gestures Reveal About Thought*, Chicago: University of Chicago Press.

—— (2000) *Language and Gesture*. Cambridge: Cambridge University Press.

Mann, S., Vrij, A. and Bull, R. (1998) 'Telling and detecting true lies', paper presented at the Eighth Annual Meeting of the European Association on Psychology and Law, Cracow, Poland, September 1998.

Marler, P. and Tenaza, R. (1977) 'Signalling behaviour of apes with special reference to vocalization', in T. A.

Sebeok (ed.) *How Animals Communicate*, Bloomington: Indiana University Press.

Mehrabian, A. and Ferris, S. R. (1967) 'Inference of attitudes from nonverbal communication in two channels', *Journal of Consulting Psychology* 31: 248–52.

Mehrabian, A. and Wiener, M. (1967) 'Decoding of inconsistent communications', *Journal of Personality and Social Psychology* 6: 109–14.

Morrel-Samuels, P. (1990) 'John Bulwer's 1644 treatise on gesture', *Semiotica* 79: 341–53.

Oldfield, R. (1963) 'Individual vocabulary and semantic currency: A preliminary study', *British Journal of Social and Clinical Psychology* 2: 122–30.

Paivio, A. (1969) 'Mental imagery in associative learning and memory', *Psychological Review* 76: 241–63.

—— (1971) *Imagery and Verbal Processes*, New York: Holt, Rinehart and Winston.

—— (1986) *Mental Representations: A Dual Coding Approach*, Oxford: Oxford University Press.

Petitto, L. A. (1988) '"Language" in the pre-linguistic child', in F. Kessel (ed.) *The Development of Language and Language Researchers: Essays in Honour of Roger Brown*, Hillsdale, NJ: Lawrence Erlbaum Associates, Inc., pp. 187–221.

Quintilian, M. (100/1902) *Quintilian institutions oratoriae*. H. Butler (trans.). London: Heinemann.

Richards, I. A. (1936) *The Philosophy of Rhetoric*, New York: Oxford University Press.

Ruesch, J. (1953) 'Synopsis of the theory of human communication', *Psychiatry* 16: 215–43.

—— (1955) 'Nonverbal language and therapy', *Psychiatry* 18: 323–30.

Sapir, E. (1927/1949) 'The unconscious patterning of behaviour in society', in D. G. Mandelbaum (ed.) *Selected Writings of Edward Sapir in Language, Culture, and Personality*, Berkeley and Los Angeles: University of California Press.

Saussure, F. de. (1916/1959) *Course in General Linguistics*, trans. W. Baskin, New York: Philosophical Library.

Scheflen, A. (1974) *How Behavior Means*, New York: Aronson.

Scheflen, A. and Scheflen, A. (1972) *Body Language and Social Order: Communication as Behavioral Control*, New York: Prentice-Hall.

Seidenberg, M. S. and Petito, L. A. (1979) 'Signing behaviour in apes: A critical review', *Cognition* 7: 177–215.

Terrace, H. S. (1979) *Nim*, New York: Knopf.

Trower, P., Bryant, B. and Argyle, M. (1978) *Social Skills and Mental Health*, London: Methuen.

Tylor, E. B. (1878) *Researches into the Early History of Mankind*, London: John Murray.

van Lawick-Goodall, J. (1971) *In the Shadow of Man*, London: Collins.

Vrij, A. (2000) *Detecting Lies and Deceit*, Chichester: Wiley.

Vrij, A. and Winkel, F. (1991) 'Cultural patterns in Dutch and Surinam nonverbal behavior: An analysis of simulated police/citizen encounters', *Journal of Nonverbal Behavior* 15: 169–84.

Vrij, A., Edward, K., Roberts, K. and Bull, R. (1999) 'Detecting deceit via criteria-based content analysis, reality monitoring and analyses of nonverbal behaviour', paper presented at the Ninth European Conference on Psychology and Law, Dublin, Ireland, July 1999.

Wilson, E. O. (1975) *Sociobiology*, Cambridge, MA: Harvard University Press.

Wundt, W. (1921/1973) *The Language of Gestures*, The Hague: Mouton.

Index

Note: page numbers in **bold** refer to diagrams/photographs.

Aarslef, H. 49
Aborigines 178
Aboudan, Rima 70, 84, 88
abstraction, images of *see* metaphoric gestures
action, gesticular descriptions of 115, 117, 126, 128–30, 132–3, 135, 147
Adele (*Big Brother* housemate) 4, 9, 149, 153–5
adjectives 94
advertising, televisual 181–92, 194–5
Alex (*Big Brother* housemate) 4, 7, 9–10
Alison (*Big Brother* housemate) 4, 5, 8, 149
Alkema, F. 28
All Saints (band) 74
alpha-males 7
altruism 155–6
ambiguity 56
American Sign Language (ASL) 24, 58, 81
Amma (*Big Brother* housemate) 14, 144, 158
ancient Greece 45–7, 193, 194
Andy (*Big Brother* housemate) 14
anger 40, 51
animal displays 60
anxiety 153
aphasia 71, 72
Appleton sisters 74
Arabic gesticulation 83, 84–8
Arabic language 84–5, 86, 87–8; verb-subject-object pattern 87, 88
Argyle, Michael 19, 21, 27–30, 33, 35, 36, 41
Aristotle 193
arm and hand movements *see* gestures
art 63
Attenborough, David 42–4
Augustus 49

Austin, G. 48
australopithecines 62

Bacon, F. 48
Barakat, Robert 83
Barnes, Rachel 16
Bateson, Gregory 22–3, 29, 53, 54
beats 159–60, 165; defining 74–5; faking 167, 170–2
Beattie, G. 70, 80, 88, 98, 104, 106–17, 122–38, 154, 180, 182–93
Beaumarchais, Pierre-Augustin Caron de 20
behaviourism 57
Better Homes (TV programme) 41–2
Big Brother (TV programme) 2–17, 36, 139, 141, 142–67, 172; *Celebrity Big Brother 2* 37, 160–7; Diary Room 153, 156, 157, 160–1; eviction process 6–7, 148–50, 153–5; first series 13–14; influence on advertising 190, 194; interest to psychologists 3; nomination process 6, 160–1; second series 14–16, 142–7, 156–60; third series 4–10, 16, 147–56; verbal communication 23
Blue (band) 73–4
body 130
Bond, C. 168
bottom-up processing 78
brain damage 71, 72
Brian (*Big Brother* housemate) 143, 144–5, 157–9
British Sign Language 24
Broca's aphasia 72
Brown, A. S. 98
Brown, Roger 98, 99–100

Bruhn, C. 168
Bryant, Bridget 19
Bubble (*Big Brother* housemate) 143, 144–5
Bull, R. 168
Bulwer, J. 47–8
Burgess, P. 28
Butler, Samuel 170
Butterworth, Brian 69–70, 94, 95, 96, 97, 103, 195

cars, TV advertising 182, 184–5, 189, **190**
Cartesianism 49
cartoon stories 67–8
Cassidy, Fran 180
cave paintings 63
Celebrity Big Brother 2 37, 160–7
children: iconic gesture development 71–2; language acquisition 175–6
chimpanzees 57–62, 64
Chomsky, Noam 54–7, 60–1, 64
Church, R. B. 72
Cicero 45, 46, 52
Cistercians 51
Claire (*Big Brother* housemate) 13–14
Clinton, Bill 139, 141–2, 170–2
Cody, M. 168
cognitive psychology 57
Colasante, C. 106
collective unconscious 52
Collett, Peter 14
communicational function of gestures 105–17, 119; description of action 115, 117, 126, 128–30, 132–3, 135, 147; direction of movement 115–17, 127–30, 132–3, 135, 137; identity 117, 123–5, 128, 129, 132, 133, 135; movement 117, 126, 128–9, 132–3, 135; nature of information communicated 109–10, 115–17, 123–30, 132–9, 142, 144, 147; relative position 115–17, 127–30, 132–3, 135, 137–8; shape 115–17, 125, 128–9, 132–6, 138; size 116–17, 125–6, 128–9, 132–3, 135, 137–8, 142; speed of movement 116–17, 126–9, 132–7, 144, 147; and viewpoint 120–1, 123–39; *see also* meaning
concealment 148, 149–50; *see also* deception

Condillac, Etienne Bonnot De 46–7, 49, 57
controlling behaviours 143–4, 148–9, 151–2, **152**
Cosmopolitan (magazine) 27
Coughlan, Jane 96–7, 98
creativity 54–6, 58; *see also* productivity
cultural assimilation 83
culture, and gestures 82–8
cybernetics 53

Darwin, Charles 61
Davis, M. 168
deaf people 49–50; *see also* sign language
Dean (*Big Brother* housemate) 143, 159–60
deception 167–72; *see also* concealment
deictics (pointing gestures) 71
'demand characteristics' 30
Demosthenes 45
Dennis, Les 160–7
deTurck, M. 168
Devoe, S. 72
diagrams 63
Diamond, Anne 161–3, 164–5
Diary Room 153, 156, 157, 160–1
Diderot, D. 49
direction of movement, gesticular indications of 115–17, 127–30, 132–3, 135, 137
'double bind' concept 22–3, 29

Ebery, Adrian 180
Edward, K. 168
Efron, David 82–3
Ekman, P. 39, 168
Elizabeth (*Big Brother* housemate) 16, 145–6, 156–7, 158–9
Ellis, Andrew 59
emblems 39
emotions, squelched 15
ethical issues 3
eviction process 6–7, 148–50, 153–5
eye contact 5–6, 35

'f. . . you' effect 30
facial expression 26, 27; micro-expressions 9–10, 14
faking gestures 167–72
Ferris, S. R. 26

Freud, Sigmund 52
Friesen, W. 39, 168

Gardner, Allen 58–9, 61
Gardner, Beatrice 58–9, 61
'gesture language' 50
gesture-speech combinations 51, 52, 63–4,
  65–72, 172, 175; analyses in the *Big
  Brother* house 143–67; analyses of Bill
  Clinton 141–2, 170–2; communicational
  function of 105–17, 120–1, 123–8, 131,
  132–9; deceptive 167–72; integrated
  nature of 131; meaning 77–8, 80, 82, 83,
  84–8, 177, 179, 180; memory for 193–4;
  semantic relationship 106; television's
  interest in 180-92, **188**, **189**, **190**, **193**,
  194–5; and viewpoint 131, 132–9; and
  word finding 95–8, 103
gestures (hand and arm movements) 1–2,
  16–17, 39–44; ancient use 45–7; beats
  74–5, 159–60, 165, 167, 170–2;
  communicational function of 105–17,
  119, 123–30, 132–9, 142, 144, 147;
  conventionalised 50–1; cultural
  influences on 82–8; disadvantages
  compared with spoken language 62;
  discrete nature 79; and emotional state
  40, 44, 51; everyday context 51–2; history
  of the study of 45–54; lack of a direct
  verbal translation 39; lack of syntax 81;
  learnt by chimps 58–62; meaning 77–88;
  as natural language 48–9; neglect of the
  study of 52–3, 54; non-standardization of
  form 79–80; pointing (deictics) 71;
  spontaneous 47; symbolic nature 78; and
  thought 1–2, 17, 36–7, 50, 69, 72, 82, 88,
  95, 139, 172, 180; and tip-of-the-tongue
  states 89–104; top-down processing 78,
  79; unconscious nature 39–40, 44; *see also*
  gesture-speech combinations; iconic
  gestures; metaphoric gestures
Gilmour, R. 28
Goldin-Meadow, Susan 71–2, 77–8, 175–6,
  177–8
Goldman-Eisler, Frieda 97, 154
grammatical objects 120, 121
Greene, J. 168

ground (metaphoric gestures) 73–4, 158,
  159, 163
Guardian, The (newspaper) 2

Hadar, Uri 94, 95, 96, 97, 103, 106
Hadiks, D. 168
hand and arm movements *see* gestures
Hanewinkel, R. 168
'Harvey Smith' emblem 39
Helen (*Big Brother* housemate) 14, 145, 158
Hewes, Gordon 61–4, 178
Hockett, Charles 20–1, 24, 54, 61, 62, 81
Hofer, E. 168
Holden, Amanda 165–6
holidays, TV advertising 182, 183–4, 187
Hopewell-Smith, Tony 180
Hytner, Jim 180

iconic gestures 65–72, 142; analyses from
  the *Big Brother* house 143–56; analyses
  from *Celebrity Big Brother* 160, 164, 165,
  166–7; anticipation of verbal content
  69–71, 72; communicative significance of
  106–17, 119, 120–1, 123–39, 148;
  concealment 148, 149–50; controlling
  143–4, 148–9, 151–2, **152**; for deliberate
  effect 69–70, 72; difference to speech 175;
  of embarrassment 146–7; and the
  evolution of speech 177–8, 179; faking
  167–70, 172; meaning 77–8, 80–2, 84–8,
  175, 177, 179, 180; non-arbitrariness
  81–2; preparation phase 69, 70, 85, 87, 94,
  96; retraction phase 69, 70, 71, 85, 87;
  sexual 150–2; span 191, **191**, **192**; and
  speech 65–72, 94, 95, 176–8, 179;
  spontaneous 81, 82; stroke phase 69,
  70–1, 85, 87; subservience to speech
  176–8; Television's interest in 180–92,
  188, **189**, **190**, **193**, 194–5; temporal
  asynchrony 72; and thought 69, 72, 82,
  88, 95, 180; three phases of 69, 70–1, 85,
  87, 94, 96; top-down conveyance of
  information 110–11; unique meaning of
  82; and viewpoint 119–39, 143, 144, 145,
  146–7; and word finding 91–2, 93–8,
  100–4
identity, gesticular indications of 117,
  123–5, 128, 129, 132, 133, 135

imitation 60
Independent Television (ITV) 180–1
Indians 51
information theory 53
interactional synchrony 5–6, 14, 40
interpersonal attitudes 29, 34, 36
intimacy 150–1, **151**, 152
Italians 82–3

Jade (*Big Brother* housemate) 4, 9, 150–2, 153
James, William 98–9
Jancovic, M. A. 72
Jewish gestures 83
joker role 7–8
Jonny (*Big Brother* housemate) 4, 7–8, 153, 155–6
Josh (*Big Brother* housemate) 14, 156–7, 158–9

Kahler, K. 168
Kalma, A. 168
Kate (*Big Brother* housemate) 8, 151; and Alex 9–10; fears of eviction 4–6, 153; response to Spencer's eviction 6–7
Kendon, Adam 25, 36, 52–4
Kohl, Helmut 141–2
Kohnken, G. 168
Kortlandt, A. 58–9, 61
Krauss, R. 106

Laing, R. D. 23
language: creativity 54–6, 58; rethinking the function of 178–9; structural levels 55–7, 59–60; *see also* gesture-speech combinations; gestures; nonverbal communication; speech
language acquisition: in chimps 57–62; and iconic gesture development 71–2; sign language 175–6
Lee (*Big Brother* housemate) 4, 9, 149
L'Epée, Abbé 49–50
Levelt, Willem 92–3, 93
Lewinsky, Monica 170–2
lexicons 81, 82
Lorraine Kelly Show (TV programme) 73–4
lying 167–72
Lyn (*Big Brother* housemate) 4

McBride, G. 178
Maclay, H. 92–3
Macmillan, Harold 69–70
McNeill, David 1, 25, 36, 65–7, 69, 72–3, 75, 77–9, 82, 91, 94–6, 99–100, 103–5, 109–11, 114–17, 119–20, 122, 130–1, 139, 175–8, 180–1, 191, 195
Mann, S. 168
meaning 77–88; American Sign Language 81; gesture-speech combinations 77–8, 80, 82, 83, 84–8, 177, 179, 180; gestures 77–88; iconic gestures 77–8, 80–2, 84–8, 175, 177, 179, 180; sentences 55–6, 78; speech 77, 81, 82, 83, 84–8, 177, 179; *see also* communicational function of gestures
Mehrabian, Albert 26–7, 29–30, 36
Mel (*Big Brother* housemate) 13–14
memory, for gesture-speech combinations 193–4
Messenger, Melinda 164–5
metaphoric gestures: analyses from the *Big Brother* house 156–9, 160–4, 165–6; defining 73–4; ground 73–4, 158, 159, 163; and thought 180; topic 73, 74, 158, 159, 163; vehicle 73, 74, 158, 159, 163
micro-expressions 9–10, 14
Miller, G. 168
mime 47
mobile phones, TV advertising 182, 185–6
Morrel-Samuels, P. 106
Morrissey, Neil 165
movement, gesticular indications of 115–17, 126–30, 132–7, 144, 147

naming 58–9
Narinder (*Big Brother* housemate) 145, 157–8
neo-Cartesianism 57
Nicholson, H. 27–8
Nick (*Big Brother* housemate) 13
Nim Chimpsky (chimp) 60
nomination process 6, 160–1
nonverbal communication 52–3, 54; conflict with verbal language 22–3, 26; dominance 25, 26–9; honesty of 22; primary function (management of social relationships) 19–20, 21–2, 23, 24, 53,

68–9; rethinking the function of 179; as same process as verbal language 35, 36; significance 25, 26–36, 69; transmission of verbal language with 24–5; unaccountability 22; vague nature 21; *see also* gesture-speech combinations; gestures
noun phrases 57, 86
nouns 93–4

O'Hair, H. 168
Oldfield, R. 93
operations, structure-dependent 56–7
oratory 47, 52
Osgood, C. E. 92–3
O'Sullivan, M. 168
Owen, Mark 160, 164

Paivio, A. 193
Paolicelli, L. 168
Paul (*Big Brother* housemate) 144–5
pauses: filled 154; silent 154; unfilled 93, 95, 96, 97
Penny (*Big Brother* housemate) 143, 144, 157–8
Perkins, Sue 161, 164, 166–7
PJ (*Big Brother* housemate) 4, 8, 9, 149; response to Spencer's eviction 6, 7; sexual encounters 150–2
politicians 72; *see also* Clinton, Bill; Kohl, Helmut; Macmillan, Harold
postural mirroring 10–11, 40
productivity 21, 25; *see also* creativity

Quintilian 47, 52, 70

real world communication 30, 33
relative position 143, 147, 169; gesticular indications of 115–17, 127–30, 132–3, 135, 137–8
repetitiveness 60
Richards, I. A. 73
Roberts, K. 168
Roman civilization 45–7
Ruesch, Jurgen 53–4

Salter, V. 27–8
Sandy (*Big Brother* housemate) 4, 8

Sapir, Edward 52
Saussure, F. de 77
Scheflen, Albert 3
Scherer, K. 168
schizophrenia 23
self-adaptors 6, 7, 161, 162, 163, 167
self-verification 7
semantic information 182, 187
sentences 95; ambiguous 56; meaning 55–6, 78; structural levels 55–7, 59–60; transformations 56
sexual encounters 150–2
Shakespeare, William 81
shape, gesticular indications of 115–17, 125, 128–9, 132–6, 138
Shovelton, Heather 80, 104, 106–17, 122–38, 154, 180, 181, 182–93, 195
sign language 49–50, 52; American Sign Language 24, 58, 81; arbitrariness 81; British Sign Language 24; for chimps 58–62; disadvantages 62; language acquisition 175–6; meaning 81
size, gesticular indications of 116–17, 125–6, 128–9, 132–3, 135, 137–8, 142
smiles 15–16; fake/asymmetrical/nervous 15–16; real 15
Sophie (*Big Brother* housemate) 4, 9
span, gesticular 191, **191**, **192**
speech 11–12; arbitrariness 20–1, 25; in the *Big Brother* house 23–4; bottom-up processing 78; communicational advantages of 62, 176; conflict with nonverbal communication 22–3, 26; design features 20–1, 25, 62, 63; difference to iconic gestures 175; displacement 21, 25; evolution 61–2, 177–8, 179; gestures as a reflection of 1, 12, 17; and iconic gestures 65–72, 94, 95, 177–8, 179; language acquisition 175–6; linear segmented quality 77, 78; meaning 77, 81, 82, 83, 84–8, 177, 179; as minimal contribution to communication 25, 26–9; origins 61–2; primary function (to carry factual/semantic meaning about the world) 19–20, 23, 24, 53; productivity 21, 25; rapid fading of 20; relative importance of 25, 26–36; triumph over sign language 176–8; vocal-auditory

channel 20, 62, 63; word finding 93, 94, 95, 97; *see also* gesture-speech combinations; voice
speed, gesticular indications of 116–17, 126–9, 132–7, 144, 147
Spencer (*Big Brother* housemate) 4, 5, 9–10, 148–9, 151; eviction 6–7
squelched emotions 15
standards of form 79–80
Stuart (*Big Brother* housemate) 14, 23–4, 143–7, 157, 158
syntax 81, 82

television 180–92, **188**, **189**, **190**, **193**, 194–5
temporal asynchrony 72
Terrace, H. S. 60
Thatcher, Margaret 83–4
thought: and gestures 1–2, 17, 36–7, 50, 139, 172; and iconic gestures 69, 72, 82, 88, 95, 180; and metaphoric gestures 180
Tim (*Big Brother* housemate) 4, 6, 7, 155–6
tip-of-the-tongue (TOT) states 89–104
top-down processing 78, 79
topic (metaphoric gestures) 73, 74, 158, 159, 163
touch 6–7; *see also* self-adaptors
transformations 56
transivity of clause 120, 121, 122–4, 130–1
Trower, Peter 19, 41
Tylor, E. B. 50

Upper Paleolithic period 63

'V sign' 39, 83–4
vehicle (metaphoric gestures) 73, 74, 158, 159, 163
verb phrases, and iconic gestures 86, 87
verbs: intransitive 120, 122, 123–4, 131; transitive 120, 121, 122–3, 124, 130–1; and word finding 93–4
viewpoints 119–39; character 119–24, 129–33, 135, 137–8, 143–7; observer 119–20, 122–4, 129–36, 138
vocal-auditory channel 20, 62, 63
voice 26; *see also* speech
von Humboldt, Wilhelm 21
Vorderman, Carol 41–2
Vrij, Aldert 168

Washoe (chimp) 58–60
Wernicke's aphasia 72
Wiener, M. 26, 72
Williams, M. 28
Wilson, E. O. 60
winking 14, 147
Witte, M. 168
word finding 91–104
word order 59–60
word-production lexicon 93
word-recognition lexicon 92–3
Wundt, W. 46, 50–1, 52

Yen, C. 168

Zaalberg, R. 168